Dear Mother

The Civil War Letters of George Washington Waterman,
39th Ohio Volunteer Infantry

George Washington Waterman

Letters compiled and edited with supplemental writings

by

Melaine Mahaffey

Cover design by Juli Peisher Rogers, r design & printing co.

ISBN: 9781693913891

ACKNOWLEDGMENTS

As I am no history scholar or professional writer/author, it required a cadre of friends and family with very specific skills to assist me in pulling together this book of George Waterman letters. I absolutely could not have done it without them and wish to profoundly thank them here.

Thank you to the Schwartz family. Frank, for amassing and caring for 200 years of family history and the desire to tell George Waterman's story. And to Frank's daughters, my friend Mary and her sisters, for entrusting me with the letters and family heirlooms, as well as the task of sharing their ancestor's story. Mary also provided essential family history through her research in family archives and Ancestry.com and her cousin Rick Sayre scoured George Waterman's pension files, discovering twelve additional letters. Rick also sleuthed his way to George's gravesite in a private family cemetery outside of Coolville, Ohio.

Thank you to historian and author Dennis M. Keesee (*Too Young to Die, Boy Soldiers of the Union Army 1861-1865*) for assisting on the writings. His research and additions were invaluable to me, and saved me from myself more than once!

Very appreciative of the long hours my sister Sharman Sayre devoted to organizing and typing George's 119 letters, to my friend and neighbor Emily Caldwell for editing the supplemental writings, and to my best buddy Joy Parker for consultation on much of the photography. Juli Peisher Rogers of r design & printing co. brought George and Sophronia to life with her book cover design.

My good friend and tech dude Clayton Jules Barbier totally saved the day by taking my jumbled pile of letters, writings, and photographs and miraculously turning them into an actual book.

And last, but not least, a very heartfelt thank you to my spouse, Bernie Adams, who has been waiting patiently for years for the dining room and ping pong tables to be free of historical collections, and for always supporting my work-related obsessions with the stories of families long gone from this world. Bernie also chose the title of the book *Dear Mother*.

Thank you one and all.

CONTENTS

FOREWORD

"Most of what historians study survives because it was purposefully kept."
— Jill Lepore, author, *These Truths*

The story of my possession of the Civil War letters of George Washington Waterman began in the fall of 2014, when, as an antiques dealer, I assisted the parents of family friend Mary Schwartz in downsizing to a smaller home. My friend's father, Frank Schwartz, a retired history teacher and genealogy devotee, was the keeper of 200 years of Schwartz and his wife Sally Montgomery's family history. In his study for many decades sat an antique oak forty-eight-drawer filing cabinet, every drawer crammed full. I hauled the cabinet

Francis (Frank) Schwartz

to my antique shop, but before selling it was entrusted by the family to carefully sort and curate the remarkable contents.

Each of the forty-eight drawers was indeed brimming with treasures: daguerreotypes, tintypes, and Civil War documents – including officer promotions and military orders. There were Grand Army of the Republic ribbons and medals, military artifacts from World War 1 and 2, old compasses, tools, rare locks and keys, and more items too numerous to mention. The most striking discoveries were Civil War items belonging to Sally Schwartz's great grandfather, Henry S. Beidler of Johnstown, Ohio. Beidler served in the Union Army for five years (1861-1866) as a corporal in the 76th O.V.I. and was promoted in 1863 to 2nd lieutenant and eventually to 1st lieutenant of the 51st U.S. Colored Infantry. Beidler also participated in forty years of Grand Army of the Republic reunions, thus amassing a large cache of Civil War memorabilia.

The sheer volume of the Beidler collection attracted most of my attention, but in one drawer was a small, wooden slide-lid box containing thirteen original Civil War letters – some penned on patriotic stationery – and a few accompanying envelopes. The young author was a Union Army private by the name of George Washington

Waterman. His letters were addressed to a Mrs. Sophronia Church, his mother. Another drawer held a cigar box of daguerreotypes and tintypes of George and his family. Frank Schwartz had enclosed notes identifying Waterman as his family ancestor from southeastern Ohio. Frank was the great-grandson of Sophronia Church's younger brother, Lewis Skeels.

Sally and Frank both died at age ninety-one in the spring and fall of 2017, respectively. After Frank's death, new historical discoveries were made, including Henry Beidler's officer's sword and a large bubble glass framed portrait of him in full uniform.

There existed one last hidden gem to be unearthed: a box of approximately ninety carefully hand-written letters, on ruled steno notebook paper. A woman named Majel Lawrence of Pompano Beach, Florida, was in the possession of and had transcribed two and a half years of George Waterman's letters written to his mother. In a large envelope dated 1959, she had mailed them to Francis Schwartz of Carroll, Ohio, with a note stating, "Good luck to you with your book."

Research of the family history explained Majel Lawrence's relationship to the family: Formerly of Athens, Ohio, her grandmother Laura Skeels was George Waterman's aunt, his mother Sophronia's sister. Laura Skeels married Moses Lawrence and their son Arthur was the father of Majel Lawrence. Included in her box were cut-out newspaper articles of family reunions in Coolville, Ohio, attended by Majel and Francis Schwartz and family. There was also correspondence between Majel and Eva Simms, George's niece, discussing family genealogy. (George's cousin Flora Skeels Hetzer was Francis Schwartz's grandmother.)

Majel Lawrence, granddaughter of George Waterman's Aunt Laura Skeels Lawrence, who transcribed 90 Waterman letters for Francis Schwartz

Now, instead of a handful of George Waterman's letters, I had what appeared to be transcribed copies of almost every letter he wrote to his mother from August 1861 until his death in February 1864. Upon his enlistment, he embarked on a faithful routine of writing two to three letters per month to his mother in Pomeroy, Ohio. He asked her to write back and suggested they both number their letters to minimize confusion and to better follow his movements. He also asked his mother to save his letters, and apologized for not doing the same with hers due to weight and limited space on long marches with heavy knapsacks.

As with many soldiers, George Waterman sensed that he was participating in a monumental and pivotal event: a war that could alter or destroy his young country. Many of the men who fought – both North and South – were aware that the letters they penned home might well be all that would survive of them, as they perished in alarming numbers from disease and battle. As generations passed on, many of these personal stories told through letters were discarded, dispersed among family members, or were destroyed in barns, attics, and damp basements. Remarkably, though, a rich body of thousands of these letters have survived, and through this book George Washington Waterman's words are preserved for eternity. His young life – given for a great cause at the tender age of twenty-three – was not sacrificed in vain. May he rest in peace and know that Francis Schwartz and family and this author are honored to have participated in the preservation of his voice through these poignant letters.

GEORGE WATERMAN FAMILY HISTORY

George Waterman, undated photo

George Waterman's mother
Sophronia Rosetta Skeels
Waterman Church

George Washington Waterman was born on January 3, 1841, in Coolville, Ohio. He was the third of eight children born to Sophronia Skeels (1816–1900) and Luther Waterman (1812–1852). George's ancestors, the Skeels and Waterman families, were emigrants of England and can be traced to New Haven and Norwich Connecticut in the late 1670s. Both of George's grandfathers, Dr. Elijah Skeels (1753–1827) of Vermont and Dr. Luther Waterman (1753–1807) of Connecticut, served as surgeons in the Revolutionary War. In the early 1800s, the sons of these two doctors, Sylvanus Skeels and Samuel Waterman, were raising their families 80 miles from one another in Lowville and Cazenovia, New York. On October 8, 1834, both of the sons purchased adjoining 80-acre plots in Troy, Ohio.

The Skeels and Watermans traveled to Ohio, bringing along with them their widowed mothers, siblings and children. George's mother,

Sophronia, wrote about her journey from New York to Ohio at sixteen years of age in November 1833. The families of two Revolutionary War surgeons were now living next to each other in Athens County, Ohio.

A letter from the nineteenth century

Saphronia Skeels makes a happy journey from Martinsburgh, New York, to Troy (Coolville, Athens County), Ohio

This young woman's account of her 1833 journey to Ohio with her family offers a snapshot of the conditions of travel at one stage of the great westward migration. It is shared with *Echoes* readers by OHS member Francis E. Schwartz, who is a great grandson of a younger brother of the writer, Saphronia R. Skeels. Saphronia Skeels was born August 3, 1816 and died February 16, 1900. The town of Troy is now called Coolville.

Troy, Athens Co.
Nov. 17th 1833

On the 19th of Sept. we started from the town of Martinsburgh, New York state for the town of Troy, Ohio state. The 20th we arrived at Rome about noon and on the 21st which was Saturday we went aboard of the Boston, an individual boat bound for Buffalo. We arrived at Buffalo the next Thursday morning (which was the 26th of Sept.) just at break of day.

On our way from Rome to Buffalo we saw many fine villages. We stopped at Rochester, a very fine city, and stayed about three hours. In that we went down to Genesee Falls to see the place where Sam Patch leaped off the falls. It is a very horrid looking place indeed.

We went through two streets of the city which were very fine, being chiefly built of brick. Just before we came to Rochester we crossed an aqueduct where the canal is built over the Genesee River, which is a great curiosity.

From Rochester we proceeded to Lockport where there is five double locks using one above the other which is a great curiosity to those who have never seen it. While one boat is going down another can be going up from the other direction. There are some very high hills in that place.

There is a bridge just before we came to Lockport which crosses the canal and is four stories high having more timber in it than any two buildings I ever saw. There was a building a few rods from this bridge which was six stories high on one side and three on the other. In the same place there was a wire foot-bridge crossed the canal with sheet iron laid on the bottom for footman to cross and all was made of wire wove in together so that a little child could cross without danger. We walked up the locks so that we had a chance to see many things in Lockport.

After we left Lockport we passed many fine villages, but I am in too much hurry to mention them. We were detained one day at Buffalo and myself and the young people that were on the boat with us went through the streets of the city and into the museum where we saw curious things. There was a great variety of vase work which was worth seeing. There was a man that weighed 730 lbs and his wife stood by his side, the most she ever weighed was ninety-six lbs. There was Charlotte Temple and her babe which looked very beautiful, likewise the Sleeping Beauties. There was all kinds of birds, beasts, serpents, shells, flies, curious stones, gold, silver, copper, brass, and all kinds of minerals, likewise a great variety of pictures, which by looking through glass were very curious and a parrot which could talk very plain.

The lake being very rough was the reason of our staying there. On Friday morning the lake being more calm we

Photograph of Saphronia R. Skeels taken in the 1890s when she was approximately seventy years old. At age seventeen, Saphronia Skeels wrote the letter quoted here, describing her family's migration to Ohio.

set sail for Cleveland. We had not gone more than three miles before we could see them vomiting on every side, some of them so sick they could scarcely take care of themselves, and infants crying, their mothers unable to take care of them. It was truly a distressing sight. We were all very sick except father, Lorenzo, and Aunt Electa.

We arrived at Cleveland Saturday evening about half past eight and had the privilege of a room (in a tavern) that had five beds in and made two of our own on the floor. We left as soon as we could dress and had to pay fifty cents.

We went aboard a line boat bound for Dresden Sunday evening. There was forty-four locks in thirty miles and there was near an hundred locks between Cleveland and Dresden on the Ohio canal. We arrived at Dresden Wednesday evening and Friday morning started on the Muskingum River for Zanesville it being fifteen miles. We arrived there Friday evening.

Zanesville is a very large and handsome city and a great deal of business is done there. There are several steam saw and grist mills, a glass factory, and a cotton factory. We stayed there until the next week a Thursday.

Sunday at ten I went to a Methodist meeting which was held in a large brick building, and at two to a Catholic vesper, and at four to the Methodist again.

Father hired two teams to bring us to this place, seventy-four miles from Zanesville, which cost twenty five dollars.

Saphronia

Sophronia's writings of her trip to Ohio in 1833 as a young girl age 16

*Lewis Skeels, Sophronia Church's
younger brother by 23 years*

Sophronia's siblings included Lorenzo (1818–1894), James (January 1820–July 1820), Laura (1821–1898), Jane (1826–1898), Henrietta (1828–1887), and the youngest, Lewis (1839–1916), born a full twenty–three years after Sophronia. As a result of their closeness in age, Lewis and George were more like friends or cousins than uncle and nephew.

Luther's sibling included Betsey Waterman (1804–1869) John Barker Waterman (1806–1845) Caroline Waterman (1816–1851), David Waterman (1820–1896), Zebulon Waterman (1823–1883) and Reuben Waterman (1828–).

Jane Skeels, Sophronia's sister

3

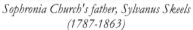

Sophronia Church's father, Sylvanus Skeels (1787-1863)

Sophronia Church's mother, Calista Skeels (1798-1876)

George's parents, Sophronia Skeels and Luther Lee Waterman, were the oldest children of Sylvanus Skeels and Samuel Waterman. They lived next to each other on the land that their fathers purchased in 1834 and were married in 1837.

Atlas of Athens County, Ohio, 1875, Troy Twp. p.83 (courtesy LoC)

*Circa 1850 daguerreotype of George (left) and his older
brother Lorin, who died at age eighteen as a result of a
fall from a bridge. This image of the two young brothers,
arm in arm, is the editor's favorite.*

Sophronia and Luther had eight children. The eldest, Wesley, born
in late 1837, lived for exactly one month. Their second child, Lorin,
was born in 1838, dying in 1856 at the age of eighteen as a result of a
fall from a bridge. George's birth in 1841 was followed by that of his
five sisters: Martha (1842–1864), Malvina (1844–1853), (Lydia 1846–
1916), Eliza (1847–1852), and Emma (1849–1946).

*George's sister Martha (Mattie)
Waterman McMaster*

5

In the spring of 1852, daughter Eliza died at the age of five and husband Luther died of tuberculosis in Brunswick, Missouri at the age of forty. Six months later oldest daughter Malvina Jane also passed away. In 1854, Sophronia remarried at age thirty-seven to Samuel Church of Pomeroy. They bore one son, Frederick (1857–1925), also known as "Little Freddy." Little Freddy was four years old when his older half–brother George enlisted, and George's many tender and loving references at the end of his letters were to him.

It is unknown how George's three young siblings died at ages one month and five and nine years of age, but infectious diseases with no knowledge of causes or cures were common and deadly in the mid–nineteenth century. Lydia and Emma were the only offspring of Luther and Sophronia to outlive their mother. Emma never married and died at age ninety–seven.

Emma Waterman, George's sister

After George's death, his official pension papers reveal his stepfather Samuel Church petitioned for George's pension. Samuel "Saul" was injured at the Foundry in Middleport in 1857 when George was sixteen years old. This injury crippled his hands and he continued to struggle to find work. He was also injured at the Pomeroy Rolling Mill. These disabilities hampered Saul's efforts to support his family until his death on December 28, 1884.

Pomeroy Rolling Mill Coal Mine.
Source Meigs County Library History Site (See:
http://history.meigslibrary.org/items/show/5705)

Found in pension petition papers, George was known to his friend, William Wilson ("Will" references in George's letters) to often speak of his mother and of it being his duty to aid his mother and sisters all he could. He wrote that prior to enlisting, George lived at home with his family when not away working and that his stepfather Samuel Church was not able bodied as a result of his injured hands. In the spring of 1861, just months before enlisting, George worked at the Lodi Saw and Grist Mill. Throughout George's letters to his mother during the war he mentioned sending and sharing his military pay.

As the Civil War left its mark on the pioneering families of Ohio, it also impacted every family member of the Watermans, Skeels, and Churches. Young men in the family were serving in the war, as were husbands of daughters and aunts. Two of George Waterman's sisters married Civil War veterans. George's younger sister Martha died in 1864 at age twenty–two, one month after marrying Union soldier William McMaster. Lydia Waterman (1846–1916) and Alonzo F. Simms (1840–1879) were married in 1870. Simms served throughout the entire Civil War, entering as a private and mustering out as a 1st lieutenant of Company D, 33rd Ohio Infantry. After returning from the war, Alonzo Simms was marshal in their hometown of Pomeroy, Ohio.

George's extended family lived in the Hocking Valley along the Ohio River. In addition to the Skeels and Watermans, the Smith, Church, Reed, Barstow, Chevalier, Hetzer and Lawrence pioneer families – all descended from a long line of patriotic Revolutionary War veterans – sent sons off to fight in the Union Army.

These letters and family keepsakes were found in the family genealogy paperwork of Francis Schwartz, an Ohio historian who passed away in October 2017. Other letters were found in George's pension papers by Rick Sayre, Francis's fourth cousin once removed, and 91 of his letters were transcribed by Majel Lawrence (1892-1967), an Ohio University graduate and librarian, whose grandmother Laura Skeels George referenced in his letters as "Aunt Lara."

*Hulda Powell Skeels, married George's
Uncle Lewis Skeels. Mother of
Flora Skeels Hetzer*

Frank Schwartz was the great-grandson of Lewis Skeels, Sophronia's youngest brother by 23 years. Lewis Skeels married Huldah Powell (1853–1915). Their daughter Flora Skeels (1876–1978) married Henry Hetzer (1878–1936). Flora and Henry's daughter Dorothy Lurene Hetzer (1904–1995) married William Schwartz (1901–1976), the father of Francis (Frank) Schwartz (1926–2017). George Waterman was Lewis Skeels' nephew.

Flora Skeels and Francis Hetzer wedding photo

After months of illness, George Waterman died of disease at Camp Dennison, Ohio, on February 1, 1864. He was twenty-three years of age and still serving in the Union Army. He was buried on the family farm near Coolville, Ohio. His letters to his mother were treasured by his family, including his cousins Majel Lawrence and Frank Schwartz, well into the twentieth and twenty-first century.

INTRODUCTION:
THE AMERICAN CIVIL WAR: 1861 – 1865

"Perhaps there never was a people more bewitched, beguiled and befooled, than we were when we drifted into the rebellion."
– Resident of the South in the third year of the Civil War.

Private George Washington Waterman

On July 4, 1861, the eighty-fourth anniversary of the Declaration of Independence, President Abraham Lincoln convened an extra session of Congress to deal with war measures. He intended to present his assessment of the United States' grave predicament resulting from recent southern state secessions, but although his paper was dated July 4 it was not read until the 5th. When delivered, it conveyed his beliefs that the country was on the precipice of a disastrous war. He wrote of the bold unfolding aggression of the Confederates including the seizure of United States government forts, arsenals, and possessions, especially within the seceding states. "Within these States all the forts, arsenals, dockyards, custom-houses, and the like, including the movable and stationary property in and about them, had been seized and were held in open hostility to this Government, excepting only Forts Pickens, Taylor, and Jefferson, on and near the Florida coast, and Fort Sumter, in Charleston Harbor, South Carolina," declared the president during his first few paragraphs. Nearing his conclusion, Lincoln also lamented that many officers of the Army and Navy had resigned, but proudly declared: "Not one common soldier or common sailor is known to have deserted his flag."

Within the lengthy message, Lincoln also explained that all peaceful means of settling the clash of politics and positions on slavery had been explored and exhausted. He even offered a peaceable solution for separation, but maintained that an event of that magnitude might be attempted lawfully only through a constitutional convention; not by treasonous secession.

The South, however, had no interest in compromise, and remained resolute to consider nothing less than complete separation as a slave-holding nation. During his March 4 inaugural address Lincoln prophetically warned of what was to come when he sternly said to southern leaders, "You can have no conflict without being yourself the aggressors."

"This trade of importing slaves," a West Jersey Quaker wrote in 1746, "is a dark gloominess hanging over the land; the consequences will be grievous to posterity."

The American slave system, in existence on the continent since the early 1600s, had been eliminated in five northern states by the 1787 drafting of the Constitution for the new republic. The framers of the Constitution, a fair number being slave holders themselves, failed to address the issue of slavery except to outlaw the international importation of slaves by the end of 1807. They also established the Three-Fifths clause, which counted each slave as three-fifths of a person for taxation purposes and congressional apportionment representation. Despite the decline of slavery in the North, demand for slave labor remained high in the agrarian South. Moreover, racism and the low status of blacks, free or slave, was intricately woven into the economic, social, and cultural fabric of the entire nation. Even while anti-slavery rumblings and talk of emancipation by abolitionists and free blacks were percolating into societal debates during the birth of the new nation, full-scale abolition movements did not begin to form until after the first quarter of the nineteenth century.

Prior to 1793, growing and harvesting cotton was a very time-consuming task creating little return on a planter's investment. That year Eli Whitney invented the cotton gin, an efficient solution to the pesky task of separating seed from plant. Almost overnight production of cotton spread from coastal areas throughout the South. The demand from England and Europe was so great cotton planting between 1820 and 1850 increased six-fold. The device increased the profitability of growing cotton and quickly enlarged the demand for slaves, reinvigorating the domestic slave trade.

International slave trading was illegal after 1807 yet the economic incentives of trading in human bondage failed to extinguish the practice. It is estimated that several hundred thousand illegally imported slaves entered the United States over the next fifty years. With cotton's new demand for slave labor in the South, the once expected slow retreat from slavery reversed itself, as did most southern anti-slavery sentiments. In the antebellum South, cotton was now the major American export and slave labor its economic engine. The South's slave population of five hundred thousand at the turn of the eighteenth century grew to four million by the start of the Civil War in 1861.

The North, on the other hand, prospered from a much more diverse, industrialized society. Smaller farms with the types of crops grown required fewer field hands, and the northerners took full advantage of cheap, plentiful European immigrant labor for its factories and canal/railroad building. As the industrial revolution gained steam in the North, also did the abolition movement gain momentum. Unfortunately, the issue of slavery was not going to disappear easily as profitability of owning slaves in the South continued to soar, leading southerners to intensify efforts to promote, legitimize, and expand slave labor.

With westward expansion, the jostling for slave versus slave-free status in the new territories petitioning for statehood intensified. The tensions and political maneuvering eventually led to the Missouri Compromise of 1820, which accepted Maine as a free state and Missouri as slave, but permanently banned slavery north of the Missouri border. The intention was to maintain the balance of power between North and South, each now possessing twelve states.

The large land acquisition from Mexico as a result of the United States' 1848 victory in the Mexican War promised once again to tip the uneasy balance between free and slave states. Civil War General and later United States President Ulysses S. Grant in his 1885 Memoirs wrote of the connection between the two wars. Grant, who had nobly served during the Mexican War although he opposed it, asserted that the actions of the colonists who settled and introduced slavery into Texas when it still belonged to Mexico were partially responsible for the Civil War. "The Southern Rebellion," he wrote, "was largely the outgrowth of the Mexican War. Nations, like individuals, are punished for their transgressions. We got our punishment in the most sanguinary and expensive war of modern times."

Following the Mexican War many northerners feared that if the northern states did not continue to compromise with the South over the recently acquired land, they would secede and expand slavery on their own, possibly into other countries and territories as well as new states. With no clear constitutional directive, another compromise was put before Congress and accepted in 1850. The Compromise of 1850 clearly calmed war rhetoric at the time, but its complex and multifaceted points only slowed the eventual coming war. The compromise admitted California as free and established popular sovereignty in deciding slave or no slavery status for the territories of Utah, Nevada, Arizona, and New Mexico when applying for statehood. It also prohibited slave trading in the District of Columbia.

The most important and controversial aspect of the Compromise were changes made to the original Fugitive Slave Law of 1793. New directives included with the 1850 Compromise stated all government officials, North or South, would legally have to arrest and hold any run-away slaves. Those not acting on the owner's behalf in returning slaves would be levied heavy fines and a person obstructing the return of any slave could be fined $1000.00 and spend six months in jail. This 1850 reinvigoration of the law compelled every citizen – North and South – to be a slave hunter and catcher and mandated the arrest of every man, woman, and child runaway throughout the country. Angering abolitionists and northerners further was the added provision that any agent retrieving a slave for a claimant would be paid ten dollars from the Treasury for each slave lawfully returned. Even if a claimant was proved not to be the legal owner, the agent would be paid five dollars for his efforts. These large sums to be paid by the government enticed many men to become full-time slave hunters. As northern legislatures took actions to circumvent the 1850 slave laws, enraged slaveholders, expecting resistance to the laws from their inception, now had one of the first excuses for disunion and rebellion in the South.

The South continued its push for the expansion of slavery in the 1850s with a victory of sorts in the passage of the Kansas Nebraska Act of 1854. This act superseded and nullified the Missouri Compromise by allowing each territory to decide the issue of slavery based on popular sovereignty. No longer was slavery restricted in new states based on location. The political goals of the South to nationalize slavery on a state-to-state basis unleashed an exodus of pro- and anti-slavery factions from elsewhere in the North and South, which poured into new states such as Kansas with the goal of voting the territory to be free or slave. These sectional hostilities led to many years of bloodshed and nefarious political schemes. "Bleeding Kansas" of 1856, as it came to be called, was one of the most contentious and violent, and was characterized as the small civil war preceding the larger one. (Kansas did eventually join the Union as a free state in 1861.)

As tensions continued during the latter part of the 1850s, the cataclysmic Supreme Court Decision of 1857, Dred Scott vs. Sandford, even further suppressed the original intent of the Missouri Compromise by once again potentially expanding slavery into all of the new territories.

Dred Scott, a slave with family, had sued for his freedom. His case moved up through courts in the states in which he and his family had resided and/or been sold into before finally landing before the U.S. Supreme Court. Chief Justice Roger B. Taney, writing for the majority in a seven-to-two decision (five of these justices were slaveholders themselves), ruled that the slave or any descendant of a slave was not a citizen, nor entitled to any legal rights afforded a citizen ("no rights which the white man was bound to respect"). The slave was property and possessed no right to sue for freedom or anything else. A ruling designed to be the final say on the status of the Negro race, the Dred Scott decision boldly declared that the slave holder now possessed full constitutional rights to take their slaves into free states and territories, and nullified all previous laws and compromises prohibiting or limiting slavery anywhere in the country. The South's cunning use of "states' rights" and sovereignty of states was greatly emboldened by the Supreme Court's decision, and further set the stage for secession.

Again, outrage in the North was widespread and fervent. The Supreme Court's decision was so reviled that a dissenting justice resigned from the court. The court's decision and its intention to finally bring the slavery question to a close instead fueled the debate and brought the nation to the brink of war.

Prior to Lincoln's electoral win in 1860, the last major event that stirred the red-hot passions of secession and rebellion was John Brown's raid on Harper's Ferry, Virginia, in 1859. Brown, a radical abolitionist who had previously participated in violence and bloodshed at the 1856 Pottawatomie Massacre in Kansas along with twenty-two others, attempted to initiate and arm a slave insurrection by capturing the federal arsenal at Harper's Ferry. The hope for a slave uprising did not materialize and the raid failed, ending with the capture of Brown and the death of two of his sons, among others. John Brown's quixotic attempt to singlehandedly free the slaves galvanized millions of people on both sides of the issue, and from the gallows his prophetic words foreshadowed what Brown knew was soon to come: "I John Brown am now quite certain that the crimes of this guilty land will never be purged away but with blood."

With the presidential election of Abraham Lincoln in 1860, leaders in the South now had the full weight of their pro-slavery propaganda to fire the passions of their people and begin to secede from a country that they did not view as their own. Alexander Stephens, the vice president of the Southern Confederacy, said this about the Confederate nation's newly adopted Constitution: "The new Constitution has put at rest for ever all the agitating questions relating to our peculiar institution, African slavery. This was the immediate cause of the late rupture and present revolution. The prevailing ideas entertained by Jefferson and most of the leading statesmen of the time of the old Constitution were that the enslavement of the African was wrong in principle socially, morally, and politically. Our new government is founded upon exactly the opposite idea; its foundations are laid, its corner stone rests, upon the great truth that the Negro is not the equal of the white man; that slavery – subordination to the white man – is his natural and normal condition. This, our new government, is the first in history of the world based upon this great philosophical, and moral truth. The great objects of humanity are best attained when there is conformity to the Creator's laws and decrees."

Confederate President Jefferson Davis declared in February 1861 that if the South's pursuit of "our separate political career" were denied, it would "remain for us with firm resolve to appeal to arms, and invoke the blessing of Providence on a just cause."

What, then, was left to be said, when the very top tier of the southern leadership put forth formally and quite clearly that in order to protect their slave system they would form their own government and most assuredly go to war, if challenged?

It was against this backdrop of dissension, violence, and momentous, cascading events that George Waterman and many young boys and men like him, North and South, came to be drawn into the conflagration known as the American Civil War.

Civil War memorial in Waterman's hometown of Pomeroy, Ohio

THE GEORGE WASHINGTON WATERMAN LETTERS

NOTE: The Waterman letters were (for the most part) typed and presented in their original form. Punctuation or lack of punctuation, misspellings and unusual sentence structure were left as George had written them, in order the preserve the vernacular of the day.

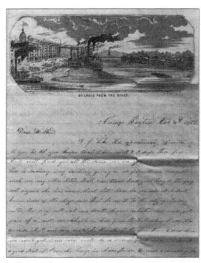

Original letter, Camp Benton, Mo. 1861

In the fall of 1861, special agent A.W. Marland of the National Post-Office Department in Washington City suggested to Ulysses S. Grant the possible benefits of a regular flow of mail to Union troops and officers in the garrisons and in the field. He believed regular mail would be essential to maintaining morale and mitigate the anxiety of soldiers separated from home and loved ones. General Grant was impressed with the idea and put forth proposals for mail to immediately follow or arrive ahead of his army on the march. This order led to an average of 250,000 military letters per day being efficiently moved throughout the country during the four years of war, and contributed to a remarkable and large body of written record of a soldier's life.

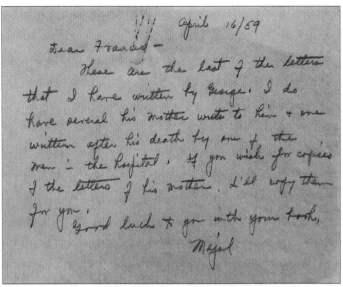

1959 note from Majel Lawrence to Frank Schwartz

George Waterman was a prolific and faithful letter writer, mostly to his mother, but he mentions correspondence with his sisters, other family members, friends at home, and friends in other Union regiments.

This book contains 117 letters, mostly written by George to his mother. There are a few penned to his sisters and several from his mother to him, and a letter from his mother home to the family when she visited George shortly before his death.

Fourteen of the letters are in their original handwriting, some with envelopes: twelve written by George and two by his mother, which were found in the Schwartz family collection. Ninety-one of the letters were transcribed by hand by Majel Lawrence, George Waterman's first cousin once removed, and mailed to Frank Schwartz in 1959. Majel Lawrence's grandmother Laura Skeels Lawrence and her sister Sophronia Skeels Waterman Church lived well into old age, dying two years apart, which might explain how the letters remained in the two families. Twelve additional letters were discovered in the archives of the Civil War and Later Pension Records of the Department Files of Veteran Affairs, National Archives, Washington, D.C., by family member Rick Sayre. Sophronia Church had petitioned the government to receive her dead son's military pension, and mailed these original letters to the government as affidavits to her needs.

The letters are in chronological order beginning August 2, 1861, and ending on January 31, 1864. To provide context to the letters, a brief synopsis of the 39th regiment's movements, engagements, and George's personal highlights precede each year's collection of letters.

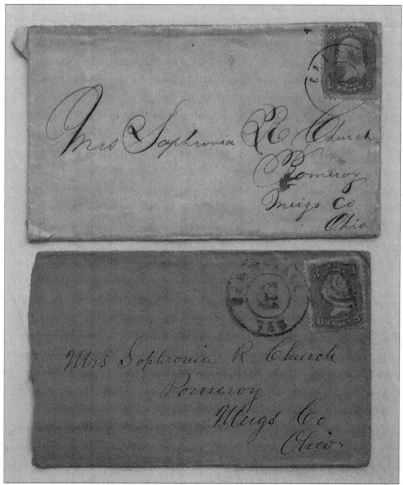

Envelopes from George's letters

4

INTRODUCTION TO THE 1861 LETTERS

"Kiss little Freddy for me."
– George W. Waterman, September 6, 1861

When President-elect Abraham Lincoln was inaugurated sixteenth President of the United States on March 4, 1861, the land was already split asunder. During his first day in office he learned through President Buchanan's Secretary of War Joseph Holt that Fort Sumter in Charleston Harbor needed twenty thousand reinforcements and supplies if Major Anderson was to maintain his post. Anderson was communicating with Washington while trying to stall his timetable of withdrawal with the Confederates. By 3:15 a.m. on April 12 negotiations had unfavorably played out. At 4:30 that morning a lone single shot from Fort Johnson arched high over the water, signaling other Confederate batteries surrounding the harbor to open fire. The solitary shell not only signaled area guns, it marked the formal start of hostilities. At last there was war.

Sumter fell two days later on the 14th, prompting President Lincoln on the 15th to ask the cabinet's permission to raise 75,000 militia. Over the next two months state after state seceded from the Union as both sides prepared for war. In early May Lincoln asked for an additional 42,000 soldiers to be raised by the different states and organized by them into regiments serving three years.

As leaders of the now warring nations built their armies, small engagements took place here and there throughout May and June. On July 21, as many of Washington's elite watched from the adjoining fields, one Union command under General Irvin McDowell met Confederate forces led by G.T. Beauregard at Manassas, Virginia, on a battlefield to be known as Bull Run. Both sides counted their losses which included 847 killed with another 4,000 wounded or missing. Little did anyone know, those numbers were small compared to what was to follow.

Lincoln's April call for individual enlistments of ninety days in duration was deemed inadequate after Bull Run. Realization the war might not be quickly won led both sides to evaluate manpower needs. Even before the horrific first large scale battle, Lincoln's July 4 message to Congress asked for 400,000 volunteers and four million dollars. Both were approved to some degree. Each state was to fill its quota of volunteers and as spring passed to summer hundreds of regiments were raised with an urgency to train and produce disciplined soldiers as quickly as possible.

Being early in the war, procuring recruits was relatively easy and thousands of young men descended upon military recruitment stands, North and South, to enlist. The majority of these young men were farmers, others merchants or small-town clerks, most of whom had never ventured far from their own counties. The average age of a soldier was twenty-five, but much younger men and even boys were eager to join the fight. At the outset of hostilities Army regulations required enlistees in the Union Army to be twenty-one. Those aged eighteen to twenty joining as soldiers for the ranks required parental permission.

One young man requiring consent was twenty-year-old George Washington Waterman of Pomeroy, Ohio. George was one of 94 recruits enlisting in Athens County for three years on June 19. Growing up in the vicinity of Coolville, he traveled there from his home in adjoining Meigs County to sign up with his many childhood friends. George and the others had joined Rhoades Railroad Guards under command and recruited by Captain John Rhoades. Their first task was helping the "Old Line," a name given to area militia units, and guarding railroad bridges in Athens and Washington County to the Ohio River. His post was guarding the Little Hocking River trestle, the largest on the line.

At last relieved from duty with the railroad George with his comrades headed to Camp Dennison near Cincinnati on August 10. Like other companies recruited in Washington and Athens County at the time, they knew they would serve under Colonel Grosebeck but had no idea what numeric designation their regiment would attain. Finally, during the evening of August 13, George, his cousin Arthur Lawrence, and the others with Captain Rhoades were mustered and designated Company K 39th Ohio Volunteer Infantry. George's new regiment was only the third Ohio three-year regiment enlisted. The cause of its early organization was due largely to Colonel John Grosebeck. A prominent Cincinnatian, he had already completed the formation of the 30th Ohio at Camp Chase in Columbus and was next asked by Governor Dennison to form the 39th. The 39th was a fine regiment for George as it had many outstanding officers including Major and later Brigadier General Edward F. Noyes, elected Governor of Ohio in 1872. That August, however, nothing was known of his officer's capabilities or where his decision to join would take him.

Little did George know what calamities had fallen on the Union Army in August 1861 near Springfield, Missouri, the same day he arrived at Dennison.

At Wilson's Creek that day Union General Nathaniel Lyon was killed, his army routed in yet another major Confederate victory. On the 13th, General John C. Fremont, now in command of the Department of the West, wrote Secretary of War Simon Cameron asking him to order Ohio's Governor Dennison to send what disposable forces he had. On the 16th Dennison complied, ordering the 39th and 27th Ohio regiments to St. Louis, Missouri, to join Fremont's forces gathering there.

As a border state, Missouri was a hotbed of blurred line citizenry of pro-Union (and a fair number of those who believed in slavery but not disunion) and Confederate minded secessionists. Up against the pro-Confederate Governor Clairborne Jackson and his supportive 50,000 state militia, General Fremont's orders were to hold the borderlands, prevent their secession, and gain control of the upper Mississippi River and its major tributaries.

By the middle of September, the youthful soldier George Waterman was at Camp Benton, near St. Louis, drilling ten hours each day. Despite the work and discipline he still enjoyed soldiering and proudly confirmed his decision to enlist in a letter to his mother, Sophronia Church. Feeling a little guilty perhaps for leaving, he attempted to assuage her doubt on her decision to grant him permission to go to war. Ever sensitive to her feelings, he implored her not to lament her actions, continuing that he would prefer being shot to being called a coward, writing, "if I die it will be in a good cause…I think just as you do[,] that is[,] I done right to volunteer." Both appeared to believe enlisting was the patriotic and proper thing to do. George's letters home to his mother and family are tender in their expressions of affection, especially for his little four-year-old brother Freddy, whom he mentions at the end of almost every letter in the early part of the war.

While nine companies of the 39th scrambled across Missouri chasing rebels throughout the remainder of 1861, Company K was detailed to stay at St. Louis guarding supplies. At last, on October 10, Captain Rhoades received orders to move to Chillicothe and in late November to Hudson, Missouri, before reaching Palmyra at years end.

5

THE 1861 LETTERS

Letter # 1

Dunbar Aug 2
11, 1861

Dear Mother,
I take this opportunity of writing a few lines to let you know that I am
well & very well satisfied with my business. The reason that I have not
written before is because I wanted to wait until we got to camp so I could
tell you where to direct but my time is out that I promised to write & so I
thought I would. We are here on the railroad. They say that we will leave
tomorrow but there is no telling. We have got ready to start so many times
& have not went that I cannot tell when we will go. But I think we will go
to Athens tomorrow & stay there a day or two & then go to Camp
Denison near Cinti. We will be there a month or two & when we get there
I will write another letter & tell you how to direct to me. They talked about
not having enough to eat but I have not been hungry yet for the want of
something to eat. Sometimes I would get a little hungry before they would
get the grub ready. When I first came here I weighed 128 lbs & I got down
to 124 & now I weigh 137 ½ & still coming up. There is not one in the
company but has gained. All we have to do is to eat and sleep ½ the time
& the other half watch. I and three other fellows have to guard the Little
Hocking Trussell, the largest Trussell on the road. It is 115 feet high. The
Capt says we will get $1.25 for every day that we stay on the railroad &
get it as soon as we get to camp. If that is so we will be doing very well. We
will be in Groesbecks regiment but what no it is I don't know. If I don't
get some money soon you will not hear from me soon for I had to borrow

some to pay for this one & paper & pen to & the fellow is waiting for the pen so I will have to stop. You will hear from me again as soon as we get in camp & then I want you to write. So no more for the present.

From your son
Geo W. Waterman
S.R.C.

Kiss little Freddy for me

Letter # 2

Camp Denison Aug 14, 1861

Dear Mother,
I take this opportunity of writing you a few lines to let you know that I am well & I hope these few lines will find you all the same. We did not leave the railroad as soon as we expected. We came to Camp Denison the 10th & we expect to leave for St. Louis next Monday if we don't get other orders and drill there a while & then go to Missouri. I like the way we fare very well so far. If we don't see no harder times we will do very well. We was sworn in the regiment yesterday evening. There was a few that would not take the oath. Harvey Pierce was one. He left on account of his mother being sick. We have to get up to roll call at 5 oclock & drill until 7 & then we have breakfast & then drill 2 hours more. Then we don't drill until evening. They say that when we have been in camp 30 days we can get a furlough for 10 days & they will let 5 off at a time. I intend to try & come home in 6 or 8 weeks if I can. If I had some money I would get my likeness taken & send to you but I cant this time for I have no money. We can get anything that we want without going out of the camp if we only have the money. One thing I am glad of & that is they don't allow them to get drunk. I have not seen a drop of whiskey since I left home. If you hear of Colonel Groesbeck's 39th Ohio regiment you may know that I am with them. It is a very poor place to write here there is so much noise. We are divided of in squads of 13 & have a shanty to sleep in & the boys are tripling about so that I don't know what I am about. We have to take turns about cooking two at a time. There is to much excitement going on to get homesick. I am cook today. I have got the meat on cooking & now sit

down to finish my letter. We got word this morning that we have to leave Saturday, day after tomorrow. Arthur & I are a going to box up our things & send them to Coolville & they will send them to Lawrences. We are found in clothes so we will not need them. I want you to write as soon as you get this for I would like to hear from home & I will answer it as soon as I can. No more at present, only kiss little Freddy for me & tell the girls to write to me. From your son

Geo W. Waterman

S.R.C.

P.S. Direct to Camp Denison 39th Ohio regiment care of Capt Rhodes & I will get it where ever I am.

Please Note: To Sister

Camp Benton, Aug 24/61

Dear Sister,

I take this opportunity of writing you a few lines to let you know that I am well at present & I hope that these few lines will find you all in good health. We are now in Camp Benton about four miles back of St. Louis. How long we will stay here I cant say. We left Camp Denison the 10th & got here the 12th. The way the soldiers is flocking in here is enough to raise the spirits of anybody. When we came here there was not but about two or three regiments here & now there is about 50 thousand within about 10 miles of here & there is a regiment comes in most every day. General Fremont says by the first of November he will have a hundred thousand men under his command. We lost three of our men while we was coming out here. One was standing up on top of the cars while they was going under a bridge & one was sitting on one of the breaks & fell down between the cars & got all cut to pieces & one of the cars run off the track & broke one mans leg so that he will not be of any account but did not hurt nobody els. We had the best kind of a time while we was comeing through Lawrenceburg. We came down that far by water from Cinta & got there just at sundown & it was a nice moon light night & the whole town was out & if you ever heard cheering it was done there. After we got on the cars & got started the cars went very slow through town & we was all waveing our handkerchiefs & a girl grabed mine & that was the last I ever *saw of it. We past Xenia about night. I knew the place as soon as we got to it. Our regiment was pronounced the best regiment that has ever passed through St. Louis & this company the best one in it. If there is a battle here we will slay the secessionists for about half of the state is for the union. I am writing by candle light and the lights have to be put out at nine oclock & it is most that time now & I have to go on guard tomorrow so I must bring my letter to a close. Write soon for this is the third letter that I have wrote & I have not heard from home yet. I will begin to think you have forgot me if you don't write soon I will come home & give you a dressing. Give my best respects to all the girls that you see. I would like to have you see a regiment when they are all out on drill & hear the brass band play. We have got a band that is a band. We drill on a great big pararia & I tell you it looks nice. Who would not be a soldier. Well I must stop. Kiss little Freddy for me. No more at present. Write soon so good bye. Direct to Camp Benton St Louis Mo 39 Ohio Regiment in care of Capt Rhodes & I will be shure to get it. Direct there until I tell you different.*

From your Brother
Geo Waterman
Mattie Waterman

Letter # 3   Note: To sister

Camp Benton
August 28, 1861

Dear Sister,
Your letter of the 21st I received last with the greatest of pleasure. Indeed I was glad to hear that you are all well. I had got a letter wrote to you but had not sent it yet so I thought I would write you a few more lines for I will have to send without paying postage & have you pay it. So I thought I would give you the worth of your money. There are so many out of money that they cant pay the postage on their letters so the major made arrangements to have the letters mailed free & paid when received. I don't like to do it but I cant help it. They say that we will be paid off next Saturday so I will be all right. You speak about my likeness. I have got it

but have got nothing to pay the postage. I got it while we was at Camp Denison. I have got my hair shingled & it made me look worse than a sick monkey as you will see when you get the likeness. If Thomas Hudson is at home tell him that I have never received that letter that he wrote to me or I would have answered before this time. Tell him where to direct to me & have him write & tell me where to direct. I was glad to hear where Will was. I intend to write to him soon for he is not very far from us. It may be I will get to see him before long. You spoke about wanting me to come home as I could. I will do that but you need not look for me yet a while, after we get well drilled & no danger of any battle soon then there is some chance for a person to get off. The way the soldiers are flocking in here is enough to make the hair stand on your head. You spoke about Uncle driving one of the government teams. I want you to tell which Uncle it is for we have more than one Uncle. I was glad to hear that mother got to go up to Grandpas. When I wrote that other letter I was in a hurry for I had to go on guard the next day & I did not write all I wanted to. I thought I would have a chance to send it the next day but did not. There was a man got shot the other night. He was drunk & undertook to run past the guard. It did not kill him but they think that he will die. I guess I will have to stop for I want to write Will more, while I have a chance. You must excuse my poor writing for I have not the chance to write here that I have at home. You get a tin plate & sit down on the ground & try it with a lead pencil. I will close by stating that I am well & hope that you all are enjoying the same blessing. No more at present.

From your affectionate brother,
Geo W. Waterman

PS The letter of our company is K

Camp Benton
September 6, 1861

Dear Mother:

I take this opportunity of writing to you to let you know that I am well at present & I hope these few lines will find you the same. There is talk of us leaving tonight or in the morning but where to we don't know yet nor we *don't know whether we will go but I think we will. Some Says that we are going to Quincy & some Jefferson City & some says Springfield & some says Washington City & that is the way the thing goes. There is none of the soldiers allowed to know when or where we are going. We have got fixed very comfortable now to what we was when we first came here. We have got into the barracks now where a fellow has a chance to turn around. They are 700 yards long by 40ft wide & one man has a bunk to himself & they are plenty large for two. I expect you would like to know (how) we fare I had forgot to tell you. I expect you have heard that the soldiers do not get enough to eat. It may be that some of them dont but we have a plenty such as it is & some to go on. We have bread meat potatoes beans rice coffee sugar & onions & if that is not enough to keep us from starving we had better go home. We waste enough meat to keep several families. I believe I will send my likeness home this time for I am afraid that I will get it broke or loose it carrying it around in my pocket & I have no place to put it. I had my hair cut & it make me look kind of slim. I am sorry that I have nothing to pay the postage on this letter but can not do it & I know that you want my likeness bad enough to pay the postage. If you get it I want you to write for it may be that it wont go the trip. We have a preacher along with us & have preaching & Sunday School every Sunday. I want you to write often for I like to hear from home as often as I can. I expect we will get paid off now soon & if we do I will send you some postage stamps. I have heard since I commenced writing that it is so about us leaving. We are going up the Mississippi River a piece & then strike out in the northern part of Ills. I go scouting around through the country, I must stop writing & begin to get ready. I will not put this in the office until just before we start so if you get it you may be shure we have gone & if you don't get it you may know that we are here yet. I will write as soon as I can & let you know where we are. I must stop now, so good bye for the present.*

From your son,
G W Waterman
Kiss little Freddy for me & tell him that I would like to see him.

Camp Benton Sept 13, 1861

Dear Mother,
I received your letter of the 8ᵗʰ about an hour ago & was very glad to hear
from you but was sorry to hear that you was not very well. I just put a
letter in the office yesterday for Martha but I am good for another one. So
here goes. It is raining in Missouri today like blazes. It has been very dry
for some time & the ground got very dusty. There is several cavalry
companies & when they get out with their horses to drill they make quite a
dust. I have seen the dust so thick that you could not see two rods from you.
Mother, I knew as well how you felt when I was at home as though you had
told me. I had no idea but you felt bad but knew that it was to late to say
anything about it, I could have got out of it while we were at Camp
Denison by stepping out before the whole regiment & had them all hooting
at me and calling me coward. Before I would have done that I would have
been shot. I dont want you to feel bad on my account at all. I intend to do
the best I can for myself & if I die it will be in a good cause. If they keep
us here much longer there will be enough here to take the whole south. It is
the belief of some of them that the thing will come to an end now soon for
the north has got her dander up now & is turning out the people by the
thousands. I think just as you do that is I done right to volunteer. It is hard
to think of leaving home for that time if it should be that we will have to.
But I have no idea that we will be out more than 8 or 9 months at the
longest. I don't think there will be any chance for to get to come home while
we are out here. They may get us in Virginia before long & then there may
be a chance to get to go home. You spoke about a towel. I don't need no
towel as long as this company stays together for Arthur Lawrence & James
Dutton and me are one & what one has the other has & they both have
towels & I use theirs. If Harvey only knew how we fared out here he
would be sorry that he did not stay with us for without joking we have the
best kind of a time. I never felt any better in my life than I do at the
present time. I did not feel very well for a few days when we first came here
but I soon got over that & have been well every since. Mattie can use my
watch and welcome if she will take good care of it. I think that I write
often enough but then I know that you wont complain about that. I intend
to write as often as I can & you must to. I did not think because you did

not write to me often that you had forgotten me. I wrote all that I could think in Martha's letter & so I will have to stop. Tell little Freddy that I think of him every day & would like to see him. I cant think of anything more to write. Who would not be a soldier.

From your dutiful son   Geo W.
Waterman
        S R C

Camp Benton. Mo Sept 26th, 1861

Dear Mother,
I received your letter of the 20th last night and was very glad to hear that you are all well. I wrote a letter to Martha & Elidia the other day but have got for another one. we are here yet in Benton & I don't know but we will stay here our three years out. There is not much prospect of us getting away soon but we are all as well off here as any where else for we have good comfortable quarters and plenty to eat and nothing much to do only to stand guard. we have guards out all the time around the camp rain or shine. I have not had to stand guard but once when it was raining and then my post was where I could go under shelter. If they find this child asleep on guard they will do well for I know the penalty is death for sleeping on guard when there is any danger. but they are not very strict now about camp for there is not danger at the present. If we have to stay here this winter we will fare very well for we will have stoves in our quarters. you mentioned about reading in a paper about the troops in this state. There is Union men enough in this state to whip all the rebels that they can bring here. you may here of our regiment being in a battle before long but you need not feel uneasy for I don't think we will be with them. I suppose you have heard of the battle of Lexington. the Union men had to surrender. this regiment was on the opposite side of the river & had no way to get across. all they could do was to stand & look as General Fremont is marching on theirs with a large force. he will lite on them like a hog on a pile of potatoes when he gets there. The quarter master of this regiment came back this morning. he said that he was taken prisoner and had to take the oath to get clear. I

expect what soldiers they have got here they intend to keep to guard the city if there should be an attack made on it. There is a great many soldiers in and about St. Louis. They consider the city perfectly safe now. There is a man to be shot today. he is a rebble spy. he owned that he was a spy; the guard caught him the other day. I have not had any letters from Will yet. I was sorry to hear that he was sick. It is very healthy here for the place. there is some in this company that has got the measles but that won't bother me any. I have not been sick any since we have been here. I never felt any better than I have lately. If you knowed how well they fed the soldiers & what a good place we have here you would feel perfectly easy as long as you knew we staid here. I feel right at home here. we have a plenty of bread pork beef beans potatoes of both kinds sweet & irish & rice onions coffee sugar & cabbage. who could not live on that. I would enjoy myself the best kind if I did not know that you felt so bad. I will take good care of myself & if I get sick we have a good doctor to take care of us. I and Arthur sticks together like two wet deer skins. we are together all the time. we have got a very civil company they are all clever fellows but I don't have much to do with any only them that came from carthay. I got that letter a few days after I wrote to you. I am glad the girls got a chance to go up to uncles. I wrote a letter to Louis about two weeks ago. I put a letter in the office this morning for Uncle William write and tell me how much you had to pay for that letter that had my likeness in.

I cannot think of any thing more to write so I will bring my letter to a close. Tell Little Freddy that I would like to give him a kiss but I am too far off. Tell him to be a good boy. my love to all of you.

   From your affectionate Son Geo. W Waterman
     S.R. Church

write as often as you can I will do the same.

        Camp Benton Oct 4, '61 (1st Oct 4)

Dear Mother,

I'll take this opportunity of writing to you to let you know that I am well and I hope these few lines will find you all the same. We are yet in Camp

Benton. There is nothing very exciting going on at present in camp. I wrote in my other letter that our Lieut. had gone to get the payroll signed. He has come back but how he made it I don't know. Some of the boys said that he went to the city yesterday with the payroll but we don't know whether we will get paid off or not. Our chaplain has gone to Columbus to see the governor about our over coats. He thinks if he goes there and sees him we will get some good coats. He is a real good man. I think a good deal of him. He brings in books for us to read. Sundays he will come around and get us all to go to Sunday school meeting. He is a first rate preacher. There is a man lives close to camp here that is a secessionist and throw out all kinds of slurs at them and the other night he got to fooling around the guards and they run him in his house and reported him to head quarters and General Curtis ordered a guard to be put around the house and not let him out. They kept him in all that night and all the next day and now they have him in prison in St. Louis. He has to appear before court martial for disloyalty. He will wish he had kept dry before he gets through with it. They say that General Fremont has been subseded by General Wool. If it is so it will make a good many soldiers say that they won't fight under no other general but Fremont and for him they will die. The whole camp was in an uproar when they heard of it. The officers did not dare say anything to them for fear of making it worse. This morning's paper states that it is not so. The report is now that our men have Lexington in their possession. Colonel Groesbeck says that he don't know whether this regiment will all get together again or not. If it don't I don't know what they will do with us unless they keep us here all the time. They say that the regiment is in Kansas City in the north part of this state. They are getting this place well fortified. They have enbankments throwed up all around this city and large cannons planted on them. They consider St. Louis safe. I feel perfectly at home here for we are all well fixed and have just any amount to eat and nothing to do. We had a little cold weather last week but it has got warm again. While it was cold we slept two in a bunk so we had one blanket to lay on and one over us which made us plenty warm. When we get our winter clothes we will be well off. In cold weather they will have the quarters boarded all year and have stoves in them. There is four divisions in each companys quarters and they will have a stove in each division so that will make it very comfortable. We are all practicing the Zouave drill most of the time now. I would not wonder if our capt intends to make Zouaves of us. That will suit the most of us. I got a letter from Lewis a few days ago. They were as well as common. Lewis was going to start to school the next day after he wrote. When you write again write what Pa intends to do in Ill. I wish that he did not have to go for I should think you would be lonesome without any of the men folks at home. If Mr. Lawrence can get any sawing to do and Pa will run the mill he may have the job if he can get what he wants to use as he goes along. Mr. Lawrence wrote that he would run the mill if he wanted him to and if he does I would sooner risk Pa with it than any one I know of. He has sold a part of our lumber at 8 dollars per thousand on the bank. When you write Will again I wish you would tell him how to direct to me and tell him to write to me. I wrote to him a good while ago and I have got no answer yet. I saw a fellow that other day that in the rolling mill a good while. He said he knows Pa and all of the Churches as well as he knows his own folks. His name was Hobbs. I believe I have wrote all that I can think if so I will bring my letter to a close. I gave 5 cents for this sheet of paper and envelope. Write as soon as you can. Tell Little Freddy that I would like to see him in the best kind. I would like to see all of you but I can't at present but I send my love to you all. No more at present. From your son Geo W Waterman S.R. Church

P.S. If Thomas Hudson is at home tell him to write to me and if he ain't tell his folks to give him the directions and have him write and I will answer it. I did not get that one he wrote. I forgot to tell you in my other letter that a man in camp Denison gave the most of the boys a testament. I have read mine about half through. I intend to read it through while I am in the army and that will be something that I have never done yet. The Preacher has give the most of us a hymn book. When I wrote to Will I directed to Point, Mo, 18th Ills. Regiment company G in care of Capt Cooper. I don't know whether that was right or not but I have not heard from him only what you have wrote. Well I suppose you see I will have to stop now soon. You must excuse me for writing so often but I can't help it I have nothing else to do. Yours truly Geo Waterman

Camp Benton Oct 4th, '61 (2nd Oct 4)

Dear Mother,
I thought that I would not seal my letter yet for it might be that I would get
one tonight and shure enough. I did and was very glad to hear from you &
to hear that you were all well. I was sorry to hear that Will was sick and
in such poor spirits. I would like to see him the best kind. I think by the
way he writes that we ain't the only company that has not been paid off.
One good thing we have tickets so we can get along. They are as good as
money when we want anything at the Sutters. We can buy all the papers &
envelopes that we want there and most of the time we can get stamps there.
You need not send me any stamps for I have not much trouble to get them.
If we get paid off soon I will send some home & send some to Will if I
can find out where to direct. I wish he were with us. I think he would soon
get well if he was here. I believe that I am 10 lbs. heavier than I was when
we first came here. You spoke about reading in a paper about the
Groesbeck regiment being in or near St. Joseph. They was there awhile but
they are now at Kansas City. I don't know whether we are counted in that
regiment or whether that have disowned us. We call ourselfs the 40 regiment
now (that is this company) You wanted me to write and tell how we fared
for food & clothing. We fare just the best kind. We have lots more than we
can eat. I wish you had all that we waste. It would keep a dozen families.
We have good warm clothes. We will get our overcoats now soon. We are as
comfortable as a nest of pigs and about as hearty. You would think so if
you would see us eat one meal. Some of the boys says that they feed us so
well here that when we go home we will starve. They say that they get better
grub here than they get at home. I am afraid the river will make you some
trouble if it keeps on. I think Mr. Horton's company is about to go up.
That Charles Pomeroy that lived in Cinci was capt of a company in this
regiment. We heard today that he is dead. They say that he died of the
typhoid fever. Well mother I think that I have give you a big dose this time.
I think I have wrote about all I can think of. My candle is about to quit
and so I will to. No more at present. From your affectionate son Geo. W.
Waterman   S R Church
P.S. They won't cheat me much in my three cents this time. I will send you
piece that came in our last paper about Fremont & it is the truth. To some

of his troops is not very well around but some of them are. Our regiment is very well armed but it was at Colonel Groesbeck's expense. The two flanking companies have rifels and the rest have the rifeled muskets. Since the regiment left this company has got hind sights put on their guns all to the expense of the Colonel Freemont all the time. It rained all night last night and still raining this morning. Well I will stop now. No more this time. G.W.W S.R.C.

Camp Benton, Mo
Oct 10, 1861

Dear Mother,
I take this opportunity of writing to you to let you know that I am well & hope these few lines will find you all the same. Here yet in Benton & I don't know when we will get away. We was the first regiment in this camp & I expect we will be the last to get away. The paper states that Price is making tracks through Kansas as fast as possible & Fremont after him. A regt. left camp this morning. I don't know where they are going. The papers states that the rebels are dissatisfied with the way Price is doing. They think if he makes a force march through Kansas that a good many of his men will leave him. Fremont is hot after him. Since I commenced writing we have received marching orders. We have to start tomorrow at 10 o'clock for Chillicothe somewhere on the Hannibal & St. Joe RR. I would not wonder if we had to guard that Rail Road. Some thinks that we are going up there to get our pay but I don't know about that I hope that is what we are going for. You better believe there was a glad set of boys when we got marching orders. We have been here so long that we have got tired of the place. There is nothing going on now to write about & I want to be getting my things together so I will bring my letter to a close. You will hear from me again as soon as we get there. I want to fill my letter so I will put an envelope in as I have a plenty of them. No more at present. Good Bye.

From your son Geo Waterman
S R Church

Chillicothe Oct 13th
1861

Dear Mother,
I take this opportunity of writing to you to let you know how & where I
am. I am well at present & I hope these few lines will find you all the
same. We left Benton the 10th about sun down & got to Hannibal at
sundown the next day. We staid on the boat that knight. The next
morning we took the cars for Chillicothe & got here about 8 oclock in the
evening. It is a nice place out here. Chillicothe is quite a town but there is
not many living in it, about half of the houses are vacant. There was a
good many secessionists here & when the soldiers came here they had to
leave. We came through a little town when we was coming out here that had
only three families living in it. They had all been run out of it by the
Union men. There is five companies of our regt here. The rest of them are
at Kansas City. I think we will go there to before long. It aint very far from
here. One of the men that was here said that we was going to St Joseph or
to Camp Benton to winter for there is good quarters in both places. One
thing certain we wont be here long for we aint needed here. Our regt has all
been paid off but this company. They think that is what we came here for.
I believe we will get our money soon. The boat that we came up the river on
is a government boat. It carried a good many troops up the Missouri river.
While it run up that river it was fired into several times. It is all full of
bullet holes. I don't think there is going to be anything done here for they
are taking the soldiers from here to Washington & Freemont has run Price
out of this state. So I don't think there will be any fighting done here soon.
When we was comeing through we met four trains of soldiers going to
Washington. The soldiers have a good deal more liberty here than they had
in camp. They will let them out here but they must not go off far or be gone
long. We have a plenty to eat here. I saw some of the nicest country out
here that I ever saw before. It was level prairie as far as I could see. If any
of the boys gets drunk here they are put on guard for thirty days strait
along or punished severely some other way. I say that is all right. I feel tired
& sleepy today having lost a good deal of sleep comeing through. I have
nothing to pay the postage on this but I thought I would write anyhow.

Write soon no more at present.

From your son
Geo W Waterman
S R C

Direct to   *Chillicothe, Mo*
                        39ᵗʰ Ohio Regt
                        Care of Capt Rhoades

Letter # 10

Chillicothe Oct 16/61

Dear Mother,
I take this opportunity of writing to you to let you know that I am well &
I hope these few lines will find you all enjoying the same. We are at
Chillicothe yet but don't expect to stay here long. We are under marching
orders & we may not be here but a few days longer. If our regiment don't
come here we may have to go where it is. We received our pay the next day
after I wrote to you. We are all right now. This morning I started $7.50
home. I would have sent more but we only got 16.20 this time. I had
drained $5.00 worth of tickets & I had to pay that & I wanted to keep
some for spending money. The next pay day will be in about the first of
next month. Then we will get our pay for what time we was on the railroad
& another month for the U.S. service. There was 10 of us sent our money
by express to Athens in the care of Mr. Baker. He will go & get it and
distribute it around. Arthur's and mine will go to the Lawrences and he
will send mine up to uncles & he can send it home by Wm Church. We
had to pay $1.25 for the package which was 12 ½ cents apiece. I could not
send much but I had more than I wanted to spend so I thought I would
send a little home. If you want it to use any of it, you are as welcome to it
as though it was your own. So pitch in if it gets there. It may be a week or
two before you get it and maybe you wont get it at all but we have a receipt
for it. All our money is in the hard truck. Have the rest of my money in
10 cent pieces made this year. Bright enough to make a persons eyes sore. If
you get that money you can pay for that paper that you borrowed & you
can lay in for a supply of paper. I like to stay here better than I do at

Benton. We fare the best kind. They sell things very cheap here. I buy milk once & a while & have a dish of bread and milk & butter to, which goes about right. The morning train that just came in brought 47 of the secession boys in. They fired on the train & wounded 4 of our men & they stoped the cars & walked out & picked up a few of them. They killed 4 or 5 of them & took 7 of them prisoners. The officers are talking of hunting winter quarters. They think we will winter at Camp Benton. Our captain said that he would not wonder if we went to Kentucky before long. Our regt has got a printing press, 5 horses & a little pony & an old double barreled shot gun that they took from the secession. Hurrah for the 39th. When we came here & went out to drill some of the other companies said the next time they went to drill they would go in the woods where we could not see them. For we was so much better drilled that they did not want us to see them drill. Hurrah for company K. There is not much news to write so I will have to stop. I don't intend to make you pay the postage any more. I would get my likeness taken if there was any artist in town. We will get our dress suit now in a few days & if I can I will get my likeness taken on tin & send it to you & let you see how we look in our dress suit. Kiss little Freddy for me. No more at present. Write soon.
From your son Geo Waterman

Chillicothe Oct 23rd/61

Dear Mother,
I take this opportunity of writing to you to let you know that I am well at present and I hope these few lines will find you all the same. I received your letter almost a week ago & would have answered it sooner but I had just wrote on the day before. We are at Chillicothe yet but I don't think we will be here much longer. It is getting to be most mighty cold weather here now. The next day after I wrote my last letter we drawed our overcoats and pants & they are the best pants that we have ever got and the only ones that was lined. Our coats are great big heavy ones. Mine comes down to almost my feet and when the collar is turned up you can't see any thing of me. We can't certainly complain of the way we are clothed. That piece that you sent me about the regiment is all true. It was well scattered but they are getting it

together as fast as possible. There is five companies of it here and I don't know where the other five is but they are together wherever they are. The place that that paper speaks about the cars being fired into is only about 15 or 20 miles from here and the place that they stopped at that night is 4 miles from here. There has no accidents happened on this road lately for they have it well guarded. You wanted me to write all the news. I expect that you get the news as soon as we do for the soldiers don't know what is going on or what is to be done unless they buy papers and we don't get any out here. Our Lieutenant got a letter from the paymaster last night and he said if he would make out a list of the names of them that was on the R.R. & them that drawed clothes he would pay them off. I think that we will get some more money now before long. Some of the boys said that the capt said we would go to Kentucky before a week but that is uncertain. I think we will spend the winter at Benton. I got a letter from Harvey Pierce the other day. He has enlisted again. He is in the 53rd Ohio regt. He said that he is satisfied but would like to be in this company. The 50th Ill. Regt came here a few days ago. They camped within sight of us. Our quartermaster said that the reason we was so well treated was because we had got a big name. He said the 39th was said to be the best regt that has passed through St. Louis. Last Sunday the Colonel had us all go to meeting. He says that after this that we will be a part of the regimental duty. When we first came to camp we drilled as much Sunday as any other day but now there is nothing of that kind going on. We have meeting every Sunday when our chaplain is with us. I am glad that pa has got into work. I expect it seems like going at his old trade to go to work on that track. I expect that it is dull times in Pomeroy now. I know it is every where we have been. This little town here looks as if it was forsaken. About half of the houses are empty. Some of the inhabitants are moving back now. There is plenty of secesh around here but they don't interfere with our business any.

I have wrote about all that I can think of so I will have to stop. You must excuse my bad writing for I have no good place to write. Write soon no more at present.

From your affectionate son, Geo Waterman

S. R. Church

P.S. Tell me if you got that letter that I wrote with the picture of St. Louis on.

Chillicothe Sunday Oct 27, 1861

My Dear Mother,

I take this opportunity of writing to you to let you know that I am well & I hope this will find you all the same. I expect Mis Lee will think that I am some for writing letters. I am sorry to hear that Will is so poorly. I wish that he could get to go home. I think that I have stood the rub very well. So far I have not been sick so as to be unfit for duty since I left home. I intend to take as good care of myself as I can & if I get sick it wont be my fault. I got a letter from Lewis the other night. They was all there. He heard that this company had been sent out as a scouting company but that is all false. They have made rules now that please me. Since we got paid off there is a good many that is drunk nearly half of their time & this morning the Lieut. said that the first man that he caught drunk he would buck & gag. I don't know whether you know what that is or not but it is a severe punishment & if they get drunk again they will get drummed out of camp & if they are caught in town without a pass signed by some of the officers they will be put in the guard house. Them is the best rules they have made yet & I do hope they will live up to them. I got that letter that you wrote while we were at Benton two days after we got there. You wanted me to get a furlough & come home when we get in winter quarters. If I can get one & come home without costing to much I will but I will have to pay my own way unless I can get the Colonel to give me a pass. You wrote that if I sent any money home you would keep it for me, if you want to use it do so. I expect we will get paid off again the last of this month which will be next Thursday & if we do you may look for some more. When I opened your letter I found a postage stamp in it. Unless you have a plenty I am sorry that you sent it for I have a plenty now. I would send you some but I expect you will get that money before you get this letter & it is about as hard to get stamps here as it is there. There was no stamps in town when we came here. I shall send all my money by express as it is the safest way. There is no news of importance to write so I will have to bring my letter to a close. You need not look for another letter for about a week as I have several yet to answer & I have wrote a letter nearly every day since we have been here. Write soon. No more at present.

From your obedient son Geo Waterman

S R Church

P.S. There is some talk of us going to Covington, Ky in them barracks to winter if we do I will make you a call. We will go somewhere soon for they cant keep soldiers in tents after the first of November.   (continued…)

Wednesday Oct 30th

As we was called off before I had time to send this letter I will tell you about our scouting trip. Sunday while I was writing we got orders to pack up & leave so we got our duds together and started. We heard there was some secessionists in a little town 20 miles from here. We went as far as Grand River about four miles from here Sunday night & camped there that night & a little before daylight we crossed the river & started for James Port. We had a great time of it every house that we came to where they had any horses we would take them. We passed one house and the Colonel let them stop to get some water & the boys went into their milk house & found a jar of preserves. I had some crackers with me & I took a notion that preserves would not go bad so I began to pile them on. We got to James Port about 3 oclock. When we got there the secesh was like the irishmans flea. They was not there. Our grub had run out when we got there & there was nothing there to eat so our Lieut told us to kill anything we could find that was fit to eat so the boys started out & before 8 oclock that night we had 6 hogs 2 sheep 82 beefs cooked. Cant starve the buckeyes. The next morning before daylight we were on our road back. We made eleven miles without stopping from James Port to Spring Hill. Our Lieut told us that when we got to Spring Hill to walk into every house & get what we wanted to eat & we did so. Every house that we went in they would say they had nothing to eat but we would tell them we knew better that they had something & we were going to have it. The boys would go right to the safe & get it. When we was coming back we burned that house where we got them preserves.

Hudson City Nov 7/61

My dear Mother,
I take this opportunity of writing to you to let you know that I am enjoying good health at present & I hope these few lines will find you all the same. We are at Hudson City 60 miles this side of Chillicothe but don't expect to be here but a few days. I think we will either go to our regt or to St Louis. There is a good deal of talk of us going to Covington. The most that makes me think we will is because the Col. lives in Cinti & he will do his best to go there. It aint as nice a place here as it is at Chillicothe nor it aint as large a town but there is more inhabitance in it. There is two towns here, one is called Mason City & the other Hudson City but they are all one town. The RR that connects the pacific & the Hannibal & St Jo RR comes in here.
There was one fellow drummed out of camp the other day for getting drunk & there will be some more drummed out if they aint careful. I am afraid there will some of our company drummed out. Every time we move there will be a mess of them drunk but they will rue it. There is some in the company that never was known to drink any before they came in the army & now they will get drunk every chance they get. Mother you may think that I may get led in the habit of drinking. You say you have confidence in me & you shall not be disappointed. If I cant return home with my character as good as it was when I left I hope I may never return. When we get our discharge from this war how will them fellows feel to see the number of times they have been drunk & how many times they have been in the guard house. I intend mine shall be so that I won't be afraid to show it to any body.
We will get paid off again in a few days & if we don't leave here before we get paid off I will get my likeness taken & send to you. The pay master went to St Joseph the day we came here. He has got a reg't there to pay off then he is coming back to pay us. I shall send some more home when we get it & I shall have a black seal put on the envelope then it will go safe. A man in this regt sent some in a letter that way & it went through safe for they never open a letter with a black seal on it for they think some body is dead. I thought I would write to you first for I thought you would be

41

frightened when you took it out of the office. I don't know whether I will send it that way or not.

A man in our company was found asleep on his post. The col said that a regimental court martial had not the power to sentence him to death & that was all that saved him. He said there was three men laying on the Potomac for the same offense therefore take warning. I tell you them words made us open our eyes. I shall look for a letter from home tonight so I will not seal this up till the mail comes in. You had better direct your letters to Benton like you did for the adjutant said we was going back there.

Write soon & excuse my bad writing for there is no good place to write no more at present.

Geo W Waterman

S. R. Church

14

Hudson City Sunday Nov 10th/61

Dear Mother,

Your most welcome letter of the 3rd came safe to hand & I now sit down to answer it. I am in good health at present & I hope these few lines will find you all the same. I put a letter in the office the day before I got yours but as I have more time to write Sundays I thought I would answer it. We are at Hudson yet but as I said before we wont be here but a few days. We expect the paymaster here tomorrow then after we are paid off I expect we will go to St. Louis. I am glad you had a good visit at Galipolis. It certainly aint as healthy in Ohio for soldiers as it is here but that is easily accounted for. You say the disease is mostly fever caused by laying on the ground. In this part of the world it never rains any. It has not rained any for nearly two months here the ground is dry & we have straw in the tents. Every man drains rations of straw the same as he does provisions & the government has it to pay for. We have not suffered any yet on account of the cold for when we have straw in the tents & have it shut up tight & our blankets & over coats over us we sleep as warm as pigs. Arthur got a letter from home the other day & they said our money went through safe. I expect you will get it before you get this. Martha said she would like to use some of it

*if I was willing. I don't care what you do with it for it did not cost me
anything. This is the first job I ever got in where we get our board clothes
& wages & do nothing. They say we will get 26 dollars the next time.
It is reported now that Fremont has taken Prices army. I hope it is so.
There was a scouting party sent out from here. They came in last evening.
They took several prisoners. One of them was a Colonel. Some say they
took a General but I don't know whether they did or not. I think by what
you said Uncle came very near smelling powder. I don't think that boat is
any more cut up than the one we came up the river on. It was all full of
holes. They carried two cannons on that boat after they got fired on.
There is quite an excitement in camp this morning. They are talking of
changing captains. They want to put the Col in for brigadier general & the
adjutant in the Cols place & change the captains around. If they do that it
will make a fuss in the camp. If Capt. Rhoades leaves this company it
wont be worth anything for they all say that they wont go under any other
Capt. but him. This is as good a company as there is in the regt & if
Capt Rhoades leaves it wont be worth anything. Some of the boys says that
the capt said that he would resign before he would leave this company. He
said at Denison that this was a good company & he would stick to it till
he died & I hope he will do it. They want to get three Ohio regts together
& have a brigade & have Col Groesbeck be brigadier general but they can
do that without changing captains. The 39th 27th & 80th is the regiments
they want to make the brigade of.
I have just come from meeting & we had the best kind of a meeting. The
preacher wanted to know why it was that the 39th had such a good name.
He said when we left Chillicothe the people said that it seemed like parting
with friends to have us leave. There was a Kansas regt there when we went
there & they was an awful set. The people all got down on them & when
we went there & behaved so well we got a very good name. Even our
enemys praised us for our good behavior.
I said in my other letter that I would get my likeness taken when we got
paid off but I don't think I will get it here for they cant take good ones
here. Martha wrote that Will was getting better. I am glad to hear it. I am
in hopes he will get better. If I knew where to direct I would write to him.
When you get that money you must get some stamps & send him some &
have him write to me. Martha said that he wanted to know when I was*

coming home. He has asked a question that I cannot answer. Tell Mrs Stivers that Wm Cole is well & has wrote two or three letters to her & has not got any answer.

I believe I have wrote about all that I can think of this time. I want you to keep all the letters that I write while I am gone. I expect you do. I keep all that I got but I have no good way to keep them clean. You must excuse my bad writing for we have no good place to write. Kiss little Freddy for me & tell him to be a good boy. I will close by signing myself your affectionate son.

Geo W Waterman

S W Church

Hudson Nov 17th/61

My Dear Mother,

I take this opportunity of writing to you to let you know that I am well & I hope these few lines will find you all enjoying the same blessing. We are here yet & I dont know when we will leave. There is some talk of us moving in the empty houses here. If we do I would not wonder if we staid here all winter. I would as soon winter in houses if we could get them with fire places in them as to go in barracks. It is getting to be cold weather here now but we have got hay in our tents which makes it very comfortable, it is too cold to write in the tents so three of us got a pass & went to a house, they let us go in & give us a table to write on. The people are very clever here, it has been so long since I have been in a house that I don't know how to sit down in a chair. Last Friday we had to go through a general review, we had to have our over coats blue pants & knap socks on. General Todd & General Prentiss was there, they said that we was the best looking troops they had seen in the servis. We done our best in drilling that day. Last night is the first time it has rained since we left Benton the ground is very dry. We have all our water hauled to us. The Union men are about to take Charleston back if they get Fort Sumpter & Moulton back it will be a great help to us. We heard that they had a fight in Ky lately and our men give them a good thrashing out. I hope it is so. We heard that they had burned Guyandotte. The secesh got up a big supper & got the union men there & when they got them together there was some secesh cavalry rushed in & killed several of them & then the Union men turned in & burned the town. That is the way we heard it. The 18^(th) regt we heard was ordered to Ky. They are trying to get all the Ohio troops there. We heard that the rest of our regt. has been ordered to St. Louis. I wish we could all get together again. They have not changed capts yet but are talking of it. Capt. Rhoades sais boys don't be uneasy wherever you go I will. I did not get the next to the last letter that you wrote. I did not get one for nearly two weeks, there has been two letters sent to me that I have not got. All I hate this cold weather is standing guard although I stand as little guard as any one in the company. Sometimes they don't call on me. Once I did not stand any guard for better than a month. My name is the last one on the roll call & they don't call it half of the time. Wm Cole got a letter from Mrs. Stivers a few days ago, she said that she would like to have him get acquainted with me if he was not. We have 9 in our tent. They are all good fellows. Arthur & I lay together, he is as good a fellow as I want to be with. When Arthur left home Mrs. Lawrence said if Arthur went she wanted me to go so we could be together.

Well I think I will have to stop as my paper is about gone. Write soon all of you. If Pa goes to Ills & needs any of that money he may have it.   G W Waterman

----

Camp Todd   Hudson Dec 1^(st) 1861

My Dear Mother

I take this opportunity of writing to you to let you know that I am enjoying good health at present & I hope these few lines will find you all the same. Your letter of the 24^(th) came to hand yesterday. I was glad to hear from you. I got a letter from Aunt Jane the same day. They were all well but grandpa. She said that he had something like the palsy, so that one side was nearly helpless. You wrote in your letter that it was snowing there when you was writing, there has not been a flake of snow fell here yet but it has been cold enough by spells. The weather is very changeable here, one day it will be very cold then again it will be very comfortable. You wanted to know how it was about standing guard. I will explain it, there is 3 reliefs of the guards. The first relief stands two hours then the 2^(nd) relief relieves them, they stand two hours then the 3*rd* relief relieves them, then the 1*st* relief comes on again. So we stand two on and four off. The guard line on three sides of the camp is not over two rods from the camp. The other side of the camp it is about a hundred yards so as to give the boys a little chance to stir around. We have about 25 or 30 yards to walk that is from one end of the beat to the other. I was on guard last night.

I wrote a letter to Will the other day & directed the same as you wrote. I think he will get it. We have not got with the rest of our regt. yet but expect to soon. There is some talk of us going to St. Joseph but that is uncertain. We are now under General Todd, he wants us to get to St. Jo but the Col don't want to go there. He wants the home guards sent there but the general said he would not give those five companies that are here for all the home guards in this state. He thinks a great deal of this regt, it has got the best name of any regt that has been through this state. If we get to go we will be apt to winter there but if we go to the rest of our regt there is no telling where we will go. They are under general Sturgis. You said it would be a great satisfaction to you if you knew that I had clothes enough to make me comfortable. I ashure you we have. At Hocking Port they made up a box of clothes & sent to some of the company. If there are any around there that is in need of clothes we can accommodate them for we have more than we want to carry around. I have two pair of pants three shirts three pair of socks two blouses & a good over coat & blanket. The Col said he was going to do the best he could for us this winter. I think he will. I think if they get up many more companies in Pomeroy there wont be many left there. I did not think Austin Hudson would hear examination. If I had been in his place I would not have went until spring. Austin got a letter from home the other day & they said Wesley & Lafayet had enlisted. Wesley went as teamster. You said that you was afraid that I would not get that letter that you directed to Benton, but they come through as well. I see that you directed the last one to Hudson but it don't make any difference which place for they will come through as soon to direct them to Benton as they will to direct them here. I am going to write to Tom Hudson before long for I would Like to hear from him. Lewis wrote that he was afraid that Arthur & I had lost that lumber where we had the mill first. He said that a fellow went to Copplegate & told him that he wanted to buy that lumber but could not pay for it till he run it so he let him have it so he got a boat of a *man the same way & the man that he got the boat of got wind of the way he was doing & went after him & found him a little above Cinti. & the man wanted to settle with him & he told him to wait till he went up on the bank & got his coat & he would & when he got up the bank he left. Well I will have to close. Write often & tell the girls to write. No more at present. My love to you all.*

Geo Waterman

SRC

Excuse me for writing with a pencil for I could not get any ink. Tell Freddy that I say that is him on the envelope.

Hudson Dec 2ⁿᵈ 1861

My Dear Mother,
As I did not get to send this letter when I wanted to I will write a few more lines. I thought when I wrote the other sheet that I would not send it till I could get a stamp but as I have no chance to get one I will have to send it without paying but I think You will be willing to pay it.
This afternoon we got orders to leave here. I think we will go to St. Joseph but I aint certain for the officers don't always tell the soldiers everything but I think there is where we will go but I think it uncertain whether we stay there long. I cant tell for certain what we will do for I have not heard the officers say anything about it.
We had quite a little snow storm last night, it commenced snowing about 9 oclock & in the morning there was about 3 inches of snow on the ground. This snow is the first snow we have had. I expect you have had more cold weather there than we have here but the wind blows harder here than it does there. I never saw the wind blow as hard as it does here. One night the wind commenced to blow & I thought it was going to blow us out of the state.
If you don't hear from me as often as you have you must not feel uneasy, for I don't know as I will have as good a chance to write as I have had but I will write as often as I can. I never wrote as many letters in my life as I have since I left home. I write a good many besides them I write home. It may be that we will not leave here for two or three days. We got orders to

leave here once before & it was counter manded the next day. There is no telling where we will go for no one has said that we were going to St. Jo. but our first Lieut & when he tells us anything, we generally calculate right the other way for he is so full of devilment that he will never tell us what is so. We are as apt to go to St. Louis as to St. Jo.

Well I have wrote about all I can think of so I will close. I don't like to send this without paying for it but I cant help it. Some days they have to pay five cents when they take them out of the office. Tell the girls to write for they have as much time as I have. Well I must close for it is getting most 9 oclock. Write soon & I will do the same.

No more at present. Good night from your son.　　　*Geo Waterman*
　　　　　　　　　　　　　　　　　　　　　　　　Sophronia Church

St. Joseph　Dec 4th/61

Dear Mother,

I take this opportunity of writing you a few lines to let you know of my whereabouts & what we are a going to do. We left Hudson the next day after I wrote & came to St. Jo. We got here about 9 oclock in the night. In the morning we start for Platt City Kansas. We are going to march through. From there we will go to St. Louis I think. It is not going to be a very hard march for we are going to have teams along to carry our knapsacks & tents so we will have nothing to carry but our guns. We will only march from 9 o'clock till 3, only 6 hours. The Col. said that his men should not carry their knapsacks. They have got this place well fortified. There is about six thousand troops here. We are camped in the station house. I am in a hurry for they are waiting on the letters. I will not have a very good chance to write till we get there. So you must not look for a letter as soon as common. If you write direct to St. Louis & then I don't expect I will get it very soon. So you need not write very often. Well, I will have to stop.

　　　　　　　　　　　　　　　　　　　Good Bye
　　　　　　　　　　　　　　　　　　　George Waterman
　　　　　　　　　　　　　　　　　　　S.C.

Chillicothe Mo Dec 19ᵗʰ/61

Dear Mother,
I expect you are anxious to hear from me by this time. Well I am still
bobing around yet. Since I last wrote we have been on a regular wild goose
chase. I wrote you a letter while we were at St Jo but I don't expect you got
it. We went from St Jo to Liberty a distance of about 45 miles. We staid
there two days then we started for Richmond and instead of that when we
got to the road that goes to Lexington we took that road and went there
first. I expect you will hear that we had a battle there for it is in the paper
now but we did not have much of a battle. But expected to have one but
could not get over the river. We fired a few shot in the town but there was
no game there so they thought it was not worth while to waste ammunition.
We killed 3 or 4 of them and knocked the corner of a brick house off &
then left for Richmond. There was the coolest set of men I ever saw. They
did not think any more of it than if it had been a shooting match. When
we had orders to load we all thought we was going into a regular battle. I
put the load in my gun as cool as ever I put a load in & then did not get a
chance to shoot it out.
We went through some as nice country as I ever saw. Liberty is as nice a
place as I have seen in Missouri and good farming country around there.
You better hope the secesh scattered when we come in to Liberty. When we
left Liberty we came on the river and kept down it all the way till we
started for the railroad. We was in the next county to Brunswick. I expect
we was not more than 10 or 15 miles from New Brunswick.
We have had the best kind of weather for marching. It rained like blazes
the 2ⁿᵈ day we was out and that is all the rain we have had. The rest of the
time it has been most delightfull weather, almost like summer. I stood the
tramp very well. I believe that I can stand as much as any of them. When
I left home I weighed 128 lbs and the day we was at St. Jo with my
overcoat on I weighed 123 1/2. I believe that I can hold my own. I have
not been sick a day yet. When we started for the R.R. it was the calculation
to go to Palmyra but when we got to Utica there was a dispatch from
General Halleck from General Prentis to go back to Glasscon on the Mo.
River & then report himself to head quarters for further orders. General
Prentis tried to get that order countermanded but could not. So tomorrow
we start for Glasscon. The general thinks we will go from there to Cairo &

I hope we will. Our five companies & five companies of the 16th Ill & a part of one of the Mo. Regts & about 6 corp of cavalry & 4 pieces of artillery form our brigade. The cavalry calls the 39th the Groesbeck grey hounds. They said that if we had marched one day more we would have run their horses down. We have our knapsacks hauled so we don't have much to carry. I will throw mine away before I will carry it. I came across John Bartlet after we had marched a day or two. He is in the 16th Ills. regt. & he is the first fellow I have seen that came from Pomeroy. Well they are waiting on the letters so I will have to close. I don't expect you will hear from me again till we are through with this march. I don't want you to feel uneasy about me for I intend to look out for No 1 & I have no way of writing while we are on the march. I will write again when we get to a stopping place & then I will tell you all about our march for I have not time now. No more at present.

My love to you all.   Geo. W. Waterman

S.R. Church

Palmyra December 25 / 61

My dear Mother,

I take this the earliest opportunity of answering your letter which I received a few days ago. I was glad to hear from you, for I had not heard from home since we left Hudson. I did not write the particulars of our march in my other letter for I had not time. We left Liberty with the intention of going to Platt City but we did not go there. The first day we marched about 12 miles & camped on Platt river. The next day we marched 20 miles & camped at Ridgley. It commenced to rain when we got most there & got the roads so muddy that we only marched 6 miles the next day & camped at Smithville on Fish River. We got there about noon & staid there that day & dried our clothes. The next day we started for Liberty a distance of 18 miles. We got there at 3 oclock by the town clock. We arrived there on Sunday & stoped there until Wed then started for Albany a distance of 18 miles. Camped there that night. Thurs we started for Richmond & went by way of Lexington 8 miles out of the way. We got to Lexington about 3 o'clock & fired a few shot in to the town & then started for Richmond 8 miles from Lexington which made in all that day 30 miles.

That is what I call soldering. We staid there until Sunday then started for Carrollton. Went 18 miles & camped at Shanghi on the Mo river with a secesh camp on the opposite side. There was several shots exchanged. One of our men got one of his fingers shot off but no further damage done. We killed three of them. Next morning we started for Carrollton a distance of 18 miles & got there about 3 oclock. We left there the next day about 9 oclock for the R.R. We marched about 17 miles that day before we could find any water so we could camp. Finely we found a place to camp & had got all ready to pitch our tents when one of the boys set the prairie a fire. Then we had to pick up our duds & go on a little further. Early next morning we started for the R.R. in fine spirits a distance of 18 miles. We arrived at Utica about 3 o'clock & camped between Chillicothe & Utica on the Grand River. When we got to Utica there was a dispatch for Prentis to march his brigade back to Glascom. He tried to get that order countermanded but could not, so we got all ready for another march when a dispatch come for us not to go. You better believe there was a glad set of boys. All of the brigade went back to St Jo but the 39th. We have taken up winter quarters here in Palmyra. We have got so that we can live in a brick house. It is an old hemp factory. The building is 100 by 60 ft, Co. K and Co. E has the 2d story. We have got bunks fixed up & 2 stoves to each company. So you can see we are agoing to live at home this winter. I would rather winter here than any other place I know of. We have nothing at all to do here for we don't drill any more. The secesh are about done away with in Mo. There wont be much more fighting done here. General Polk come & give them heck at Lexington a few days after we was there. He got back very near all the guns that we lost when Mulligan surrendered there. We took a prisoner at Smithville that was in Price's army. He was Price's cannoneer. We kept him with us till we got to the RR then they let him off on Parol of honor. He came to Capt Rhoades & wanted to join this co. So we took him in. He says that Price has not many men now. Our capt says that we will all get to go home in the spring. I do hope we will. I got a letter from Will a few days ago. He is well. He sent me 5 stamps & I got a letter from you the same day with 6 more in it. I expect we will get paid off in a few days. Well will have to stop. You may now direct your letters to Palmyra for we will be here some time.

From your son George Waterman

6

INTRODUCTION TO THE 1862 LETTERS

"You wrote in your letter for me not to get caught stealing chickens or milking cows. I have not stole any chickens, but I did milk a cow."
– George W. Waterman, January 11, 1862 (Palmyra, Missouri)

On January 1, 1862, Co. K and two others of the 39th Ohio were billeted at Palmyra, Missouri, in a two-story hemp factory, a good spot with the cold of winter ahead. George started the year writing letters home to mother Sophronia with his first written on January 3, his twenty-first birthday. In this first missive of the year he relayed disturbing news concerning theft by fellow soldiers from the building including whiskey, blankets, cigars, cheese, and candy. Most, including George, did not participate in the theft, but the quartermaster's office was trying to have the entire regiment assessed three thousand dollars in damages. George vigorously maintained it was a gross over-charge for the actual value of items stolen, and did not count out blowing the whistle on those who stole, if the assessment was levied. The ordeal was a hard lesson in unintended consequences for the young men of the 39th.

The new year also saw the continuance of Missouri "secesh" destroying railroads and bridges, besides harassing and engaging the Army of the West at every chance. Major General Henry W. Halleck was now commanding the western armies following President Lincoln's removal of General Fremont for insubordination in November. Halleck's no-nonsense command style demanded much from his men as they continued pushing insurgents out of the state. His intent was to bring order to Missouri as fast as possible so western commanders could direct their full attention to advancing on Rebel strongholds on the Mississippi, Tennessee, and Cumberland rivers.

Control of the major western rivers would secure the most favorable transport route for the army's supplies as well as help to control events in the border states of Kentucky and Missouri, slave states that had not seceded.

On January 29, Special Order Number 29 arrived at Headquarters, District of the Missouri from General Pope commanding, directing the army to move. At last the majority of scattered Union forces within the state were to unite at St. Louis. In mid-February, soon after George and the men of Company K arrived, the rest of the regiment also came into camp and the 39th Ohio was together for the first time in many months. Upon arrival many who endured the harsh marching conditions cried out, "from mud we came, to mud we return."

While Pope's army struggled with cold and mud marching to Camp Benton at St. Louis during February, the Army of the Tennessee commanded by General Ulysses S. Grant and the Mississippi River Squadron under Flag Officer Andrew H. Foote elated northern spirits by capturing Fort Henry on the Tennessee River and soon after Fort Donelson on the Cumberland River, opening the way to Nashville. Their demise was a severe blow to the Confederates' control of Tennessee and parts of Kentucky.

On February 25 at Commerce, Missouri, the 39th Ohio was joined with the 27th, 43rd, and 63rd Ohio Infantry regiments under command of Colonel John W. Fuller of the 27th. The four regiments would serve together throughout the war proudly as Fuller's Ohio Brigade. On the 28th, the new brigade commenced a fifty-mile march through swampy lands into the "sunk country" surrounding New Madrid, Missouri on the Kentucky border.

On March 3 with the Ohio Brigade in advance, the army halted in a corn field one half mile from the town. The Confederates fired from their gun boats on the Mississippi River and also their fort on the riverbank at Madrid Landing at the mass of approaching soldiers, prompting a short distance withdrawal as night arrived. After jockeying around the town for the next ten days, the Federals at last advanced toward the fort on the 14th. It was the 39th's first time under fire which left a big impression on George, who wrote home of the "little knock down," on March 15 and in greater detail on the 17th.

The campaign's next goal was the capture of Island No. 10, so named because it was the tenth island south of the Ohio River. Its strategic location on the Mississippi, where the river went into a double curve, created a bottleneck to attack or trap the Union Navy from infiltrating the South. Upon it the Confederates had erected another fort which had to be taken. George and the 39th stayed at New Madrid, receiving orders to move and not move for the rest of March. Finally, on April 7, the regiment moved across the river to cut off Confederates attempting to leave the island. On the 8th, Island No. 10 fell, motivating George to write a lengthy and insightful letter home once again.

While the Ohio Brigade as part of General Pope's Army of the Mississippi took part in the capture of Island No. 10, General Grant's Army of the Tennessee narrowly avoided disaster with the timely arrival of General Buell's Army of the Ohio at Pittsburg Landing, Tennessee, on the battlefield forever known as Shiloh. The April 6 and 7 struggle caused the Confederates to withdraw to Corinth, Mississippi, an important rail town.

Ever keeping up on the war in general, George's occasional mentions of Major General Ulysses S. Grant, the eventual lieutenant general of the entire Union Army, were surprisingly unfavorable during this period. He clearly expressed a lack of interest in serving under Grant when writing home. This was most probably due to negative and what was eventually deemed unfair press coverage General Grant received from northern newspapers after Shiloh.

The Confederate retreat from Pittsburg Landing to Corinth in April would eventually hugely impact the 39th and Fuller's Brigade in general. Before the month passed the Army of the Mississippi was laying siege to the town. After a long struggle for control of Corinth, the Confederates at last left on May 30. George's June 8 letter proudly described his regiment's part, proclaiming they planted the first Union flag on the courthouse. Throughout the next few months, George stayed at Corinth, sometimes driving the wagons as a teamster. His depleted health caused him mainly to stay in camp. On September 19 his command participated in the battle of Iuka and on October 3 and 4 the Battle of Corinth as the Rebel army had returned to retake the town. Fortunately for George he was not on the line at Battery Robinett where his beloved Company K was entrenched. During the course of the two-day engagement the brigade lost 51 killed and another 261 wounded.

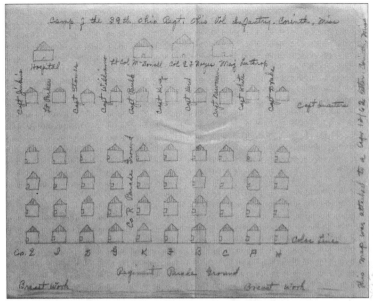

Map of 39th regiment camp, Corinth, Mississippi

In November the 39th Ohio was transferred to the 13th Corps as part of the Department of the Tennessee. Despite his misgivings, the change of command meant George was under command of Major General Grant.

Throughout 1862, George continued writing home, his letters fluctuating in length. Now immersed in war, he recounts numerous interactions with southerners, including punishments for not cooperating with the invading army. "That is the way Lincolnites treats them when they get too saucy," he wrote. He shares openly the story of a man hiding in a tree suspected of robbing people who was promptly given a "secesh pill" by a member of the regiment; shot and killed while sitting upon his perch.

The reader also begins to sense the waning of the excitement of soldiering, as George writes to his mother in July 1862, "One year ago today I (very patriotically) [sic] went up to Cutter Station & enlisted but I ain't half as Patriotic now as I was then…I have commenced to help put this rebellion down and I will see the end of it if I live that long…when I take another oath I will understand the nature of it before I take it."

The Waterman letters of 1862 reflect a seesaw of emotions, victories in the West, and optimism that the Rebels were almost played out, followed by discouragement over losses in the East and despair that there was no real end in sight for this protracted bloody war. In addition, George's general good health was beginning to decline, with the first mentions of bouts of chronic diarrhea in September. His frustration with the generals and slow progress of the war were clearly expressed. At the close of 1862 he had now been away from home for one year and five months.

THE 1862 LETTERS

Palmyra, My Birthday, 1862
(Jan.3rd.)

My Dear Mother,
*I take this opportunity of writing you a few lines to let you know that I am
in most excellent health & I hope these few lines may find you all the same.
We are having very easy and comfortable times here now.*
*I am very glad we did not take that other march for it has been very cold
since we got back. We had most beautiful weather while we was on the
march & the very day we got back it commenced to get cold and it has been
cold ever since. Our regt has had a very good name ever since it came out
but I am afraid it will get a hard name now for while we were at St. Jo we
quartered in the station house & the boys stole some blankets & cheese
cigars candy & whiskey. The other day a bill of $3000 damage came to
our quartermaster & he would not accept of it & so they sent it to
Washington City. I don't know what will be done about it. 3 thousand
dollars is five times the worth of the things that was taken. There was only
three companies in there and they could not carry $3000 worth of the
things that was there. One thing certain I did not take a single thing. There
was a barrel of whiskey in there that the boys had taped & half of the
boys filled their canteens with it but I did not even smell of the stuff but if
we have to pay for it one will have to pay as much as the other. If they get
anything out of me they will have to stop my pay for if I have the names I
want the game. They all say they won't pay anything. We expect to get paid
off the 10th of this month. We will get 4 months wages when we do get it. I
don't expect to send much home this time for I want to keep more than I*

did before. I owe Lafayet Milchel some & he wants it & I am going to get me a revolver if it costs me a lawsuit for a person needs one here. We stand police guard here just the same as a policeman. All we have to do is to keep the boys from doing any damage to the property in town and if we find any of the boys drunk we have to take them to the guard house. We had quite a spot of fun with a couple of citizens the other day for selling whiskey to the soldiers. They had been warned not to sell the soldiers any whiskey but they would do it so they took a couple of the rum sellers and got two barrels and cut a hole through the bottom of it and put them over their heads and wrote on the outside of the barrels in great big letters Sold bad whiskey to the Soldiers. They marched them all through town with them barrels on their shoulders. I don't expect the 39th will ever get together again. They say the other half of the regt has went into an artillery regt. Some says that the col. Said that he would disband but I don't think he can. I think he will have to go to camp and recruit. There is a good deal of talk of England helping the South but I have no fears of that. The late papers think that there is nothing of it. We have enough men in the field to whip the South in one months time if they would only go at it but I think that this war is a kind of speculation & the head men are holding it off as long as they can so as to make all they can. Arthur got a letter from home the other day & they said that Mr. L. had moved our mill up there. They set it on Wesley's place where Kinney mill set. I wish it was so Pa could run it. Arthur said he would rather give him $3 a day than have a green hand run it. If you see any of Stivers folk tell them Wm Cole is well. He is one of our cooks now. We have two cooking stoves & have the company divided and two cooks to each part. Wm is a first rate fellow. I like him very well. I shall have to stop. Write often. My love to you all.

G.W.W.
S.R.C.

Palmyra Mo. Jan 11/62

My dear Mother.
I take this opportunity of writing you a few lines to let you know that I am in excellent health & hope these few lines may find you all the same.

I have not had a letter from home since Christmas. I think there is one on the way for me but likely it has been detained some way. The secesh has been destroying the RR so that the cars don't run regular. They burned every bridge for 100 miles on the North Mo road & that is the way the mail has to come. We have got 5 or 6 prisoners here that was caught destroying the RR. General Halleck's orders is to shoot all that is caught destroying the RR or Telegraph. I hope they will shoot them & that will be a warning to the rest. They say that those prisoners we have got are sentenced to be shot but I don't know.

All the guarding we have to do now is to guard the prisoners. They took 30 of them to St. Louis this morning so it wont take so many guards now. We will get our pay today or tomorrow. The paymaster has been here a day or two & he is going to commence to pay this morning. We will be the last comp paid so we will not get it till tomorrow as they cant pay five comps in one day. Our Capt is going home on a furlough when he gets his pay & I shall send some to Lafayet Mitchell by him if he goes.

I got two letters from Will the other day. He said that he wished he was in this camp for he don't like his Regt. He says that the Col & Lieut Col & the Major is under arrest. He says that he is going to try & get a transfer to this comp. He cant get in any better Regt than this. I wish it was altogether but I don't expect it will be soon. One half of it is under General Sturgis & the other under Prentis. Sturgis offers two regts of Mo troops for this half but Prentis wont let us go. Prentis offers one regt for the other half & Sturgis wont let them go. I think that one general ought to have the whole Regt but neither one of them are willing to give their half up.

I got a letter from Uncle Moses yesterday. They were all well. Our chaplain went to Columbus some time ago to get our waist coats & caps but he has not got back yet. I expect it is on account of the RR being destroyed. You wrote in your other letter for me not to be caught stealing chickens or milking cows. I have not stole any chickens but I did milk a cow while we was on the R.R. There was a good many chickens stole while we was on that march but I did not steal any. You said that Jim Davis was going to write to me. I have not got any letter from him yet. Tell Mattie if she wants to write to Adaline Dudery to direct to Jeffersonville Wayne Co Ill. Will told me where to direct, I don't know as I have anything more to write that will be interesting. Tell little Freddy that I would like to see him the best kind. Well I guess I will have to close. Write as often as you can & I will do the same. No more this time.

From your son
Geo Waterman
S R Church

26

Palmyra, Marion Co, Mo.
Jan 31st 1862

My dear Mother,
Your letter of the 20th came safe to hand this morning. I was very glad to hear from home for it had been over two weeks since I had heard from home but I expected it was on account of the high water. I heard in some of the boys letters that the river was very high. I expected it would be in our house. About half of the boys in this camp have got the mumps. A flesheyer set of boys you never saw. I think it curious that I don't take them for I don't know that I ever had them. I am helping Wm. Cole cook now for the fellow that was helping him has got the mumps so I don't get to write whenever I want to.
The paper states that Prices men are all disbanding & coming home. His army of 40,000 men that he had last summer is reduced down to about 10,000 a good many of his are from (8 about) this place. Every few days there is a lot of Prices men comes home & as soon as they get here we take them & them that will take the oath they let go & them that don't we send to St Louis to work on the fortifications. They have taxed the people of this county for the bridges that the secesh have destroyed. I tell you the citizens of this place is wealthy (?). Secesh is about played out in the northern part of this state. If there is any more fighting done in this state it will be on the other side of the Mo. River & we will not go on the other side of the river as long as we are under general Prentis for he is not allowed to go on the other side of the river. I don't think this war will last much longer for about all the south had to look to was England & that

has all played out now.

There is 8 of the prisoners that we have here sentenced to be shot for burning bridges & destroying the RR. It looks hard to shoot a man but I don't know as it is any worse than for them to destroy a bridge & may be put thousands of lives at stake.

Our capt tried to get a furlough to go home but could not get one & he is going to resign if he can. I hope he wont leave us for he is such a good Capt. We wont get another capt like him. You wanted me to write & tell you how I get along for clothes & how we fare. Well we have all we want to eat & wear. Every week or two our orderly Sargent finds out who wants clothe & what they want so we have a chance to draw clothes whenever we want too. I have had a cold for 3 or 4 days & it aches a little tonight so I guess I will not write much more tonight. I want to write some to the girls in this letter so I will not send it out by this mail. Tell little Freddy that I think of him every day & would like to see him the best kind. No more this time.

from your son Geo Waterman
S R Church

Palmyra Marion Co. Mo.
Feb 6th 1862

My Dear Mother,

I now seat myself with the intention of writing you a letter & you will think it is a letter before I get done. In the first place I am enjoying excellent health & hope these few lines may find you enjoying the same. I am still helping to cook & therefore don't get much time to write. I have been cooking over two weeks but don't expect to cook much longer. While we are cooking we are exempt from all other duty. I have not been on guard for a good while. I haven't had a letter from Will for some time. I used to get a letter every week from him before the high water. I would not wonder if their Regt had left Cairo for I see in the papers that several Regiments had left there but did not tell what ones but was believed that some important victory would be won before they returned. I believe there will be something done before long for they are sending a good many troops to Cairo. The 16th

Ills went there not long ago & it is believed that we will go there or to Kentucky before long but it is uncertain for the Cavalry that are here have marching orders & if they leave here we will stay until some other troops comes in to take our place. I expect our Regt will be united before long now. The Chaplain got a letter from the other part of the Regt & they was then marching this way with ten days rations with them.

A fellow in Co went to the Col the other day to get a transfer to go on a gun boat & the col told him that it was not worth while to get a transfer for we would not be in the service a year & that he had better stay in the Regt while he was in it for if he went off & could not get on a gun boat we would be gone by the time he got back. He said we would be in Cairo in less than three weeks. I don't know whether the Col meant that we would not be in the servis a year to come or a year from the time of our enlistments. But one thing certain I expect to be at home before a year from now if I live that long. A little incident occurred the other day that I will relate. While a few of Col More's men were scouting around through the country they spied a man up in the top of a very high tree, he had a musket & a revolver & they thought he had no very urgent business up there & that he had better come down. So one of the men let drive & put a secesh pill right his head & down he come through the limbs on the ground. They examined him & found that he had a plenty of money about him. I forgot the amount they got all in gold & silver. It is supposed that he was there to kill any person that come along there that had any money. I think that is the way he came by so much money. That is about the way the secesh generaly works in this country. They go sneaking about in the bushes & if a half of the number of men that they have got comes along they will shoot once & then run. That's the way they fight here. Well I will have to stop for the present. To be continued.

Chapter 2.   *Friday the 7th*

As I have a little time now I will try to write some more. I don't intend to send this out until I get a letter from home which I look for in this mail. We have just heard that Fort Henry is taken by our men. How true it is I don't know but I do sincerely hope it is so. There was some talk of us going to Tennessee but that is all died away now. But I think we will go to Ky before long or to Cairo for there is nothing to do in this state any more. We may have to stay in this place till next summer for all I know. One thing certain we will not go in any better place if we leave here. We have good quarters here & all the privilidge that we want to run around. The boys are in fine spirits now. They are cutting around & making more noise than a dozen such families as Hudsons can. When I come home I don't believe I can sleep unless there is some noise for I have got so used to it that the more noise there is the sooner I can go to sleep. The boys have got about over the mumps but I did not happen to take them. I intend to send Pa a Palmyra Courier. There is a good deal of reading in it for a little paper. You will see in the paper that I shall send the way Benett Davis (our orderly sargent) directed a letter to his mother. He is about as smart a fellow as I ever saw if he would only let his smartness run the right way it would do him some good. Well it is too dark to write more so I will stop for this time.

Chapter 3   *Saturday Morning Feb 8th*

I now seat myself to write some more & expect it will be the last letter that I will write in Palmyra for in the morning we start for the noble state of Ky. Thank fortune we are going to leave Mo. We are first going to Benton & stay there till we get some more clothes & we are to meet the other part of the Regt there & then go to old Ky. We are all well pleased with the movement. I expect we will go by Cairo & may be we will stay there a while & if the 18th Ill is there I will get to see Will. I had an idea that we would leave this state before long for there is nothing to do here. We got a dispatch late last evening that it is so about Fort Henry being taken by our men. When the chaplain came in & told us of it. Such yelling you never heard as there was made here.

I got a letter last evening from Lewis & Jane. They were as well as usual. Arthur got a letter from his father & he said that Blandy (the man we got the mill of) was going to take the mill back for what is comeing to him. Arthur thinks it is best to let them have it back if they will give up all claims that they hold against him. If they take the mill back we will have nothing to do when we get back. We are all busy now getting ready to leave & I have not much time to write. I did intend to fill this full but I don't know as I will now for I will be very busy now getting ready to leave. You will hear from me again when we get to Benton. No more at present but remain your obedient son.   Geo W. Waterman

S R Church

P.S. There is a man to be drummed out of camp this afternoon for stealing a pair of boots. I could write a good deal more if I had time. My best respects to all enquiring friends.

Geo

Palmyra, Marion Co. Mo
Feb 10, 1862

My Dear Mother,
Your most welcome letter of the 2d came safe to hand this evening. I was very glad to hear from you & to hear that you was all well. I expect you will think strange me writing as I do but we had orders to leave here but not as soon as I wrote by two days. we had orders this morning to cook rations enough to last us to St Louis & not more than three hours after that the order was countermanded. that is the way it goes. we don't know one hour what we will do the next, I wish we had went now for it is such nice weather here now. it seems almost like spring. all the time you was haveing so much rain there we was having snow here. we arrived here the 20th of Dec & we had not been here more than two hours when it commenced to snow & there has been snow on the ground ever since but it is going off very fast now. you say that it is a great comfort to you to get letters from me. I know it is & that is the reason why I write so often. I would not do the least thing that would be displeasing to you if I could help it. there are several in this comp. that never drank liquor when they were at home & now they will drink it whenever they can get it. I am glad to say that I am not one of them. I often think when I see them drinking how their mothers would feel if they knew of it & more than that I have thought how my mother would feel to know that her son was a drunkard but I know you have confidence enough in me to know that I will never be the case.
the people here thinks there never was another such a Regt as this. some of them actualy cried when we got marching orders. The Col. said the other day that we was going to leave here & he wanted us to leave like men for we had got a good name here & he wanted us to take our good name with us. he said that we had got a better name than we deserved & that is so for

there is some as hard cases in this Regt as there is in any Regt. but where will you find a Regt of men take them as they come but what there will be some hard cases among them. as a general thing this is the best Regt that I have seen yet. I was at meeting last evening & the best kind of a one too. the preacher said the 39ᵗʰ had set an example while here for them to follow. you wanted to know what denomination our chaplain belongs to. I think he is a Presbyterian. I wish you could hear him preach once for I know it would do you good to hear him. I would rather hear him preach than any body I ever heard. I was very glad to get that paper for it seemed so much like home to read it. we have papers to read all the time here but they aint from home. I had a mind to take the Palmyra Courier 4 months & send to Pa but I have not the money to spare. I could get it for 50 cts for 4 months & I know Pa would like to read it but I expect after we leave it will not be as interesting to you for it had a good deal to say about this Regt. you spoke about me geting my next likeness taken in my dress suit. we have not got it yet but expect to when we get to St. Louis. then I will try & get it but I wont have as good a chance there as I will here. I am glad you all liked the one I sent. I think it is a good one. I want to answer Mattie's letter this evening so I will have to close. My love to all of you. no more this time but remain your obedient son.   G.W. Waterman

S K

Church

excuse my bad writing for I have a poor pen & a poor place to write.

Camp Benton, Mo
Feb 14ᵗʰ 1862

Dear Mother.
After a long but pleasant trip we find ourselves in old Benton again. We left Palmyra the next day after I wrote my last letter. we had most beautiful weather for our trip but it commenced to snow as soon as we got here & there is about four inches of snow on the ground now. We left Palmyra about daylight on Wednesday & got to Hudson about noon. there we changed cars & got started about 3 oclock from there & got to St. Charles about two oclock, in the night. we stayed on the cars till morning then

crossed the river & took the cars again for St. Louis & got there about
noon & then marched out to camp & of all muddy places ever I saw
Benton beat all but it is the same old Benton yet.

The other part of our regiment will be here in a few days & next Monday
or Tuesday we start for Ky. I expect we will go by water & very likely we
will stay at Cairo a while. It is not decided whether we will go to Ky or
Tenn. we will go up the Cumberland or Tennessee river. we will get some
more clothes in a few days. we had passenger cars all the way through. The
Col said his men should have good cars for they was coming out in every
respect. the conductor told him that some of the men could ride on the
freight cars. no they cant says the Col you will get two more box cars &
then we will go through like a town clock. the old Cols head is right if he
did fall in the mud. another victory won. our men has taken Ronoke
island. I think the rebels will give before long. the next fight I think will be
at Columbus. I will send you some pictures. they are all very natural. the
fair ground would be nice to put in a frame. well Mother I have a poor
place to write & it is so cold that I cant hardly write so you must excuse my
short letter. you will hear from me soon. I will close by stating that I am in
excellent health & hope these few lines may find you all the same. Your son
George

        S R Church

29

                    Benton, Feb 19th 62

Dear Mother
our capt is going home & he will draw our RR money & I shall have him
put mine in this & send it home. I would have it sent back to me but we
will be gone from here before it could get back & then I might lose it. our
capt has resigned his commission & will leave in a few days. I expect Lieut
Paulk will be our capt. I am on guard today & have not time to write
much. I thought I would have my money sent home & if I need any before
we get paid off again I will have you send me some.

               Your son Geo Waterman

S R Church

Camp Benton
Feb 20/62

Dear Mother
I now seat myself to write you a few lines to let you know that I am still among the living & enjoying good health & hope these few lines will find you the same.
The other part of our Regt came here yesterday so the 39 is once more a whole Regt. & starts tomorrow or next day for Memphis Ten. that just suits us. we got two of the nicest flags today that I ever saw, one American flag & a Regimental flag. the two cost $110.00
we got a new uniform today all but our waist coats. we wont get them for a while yet. we got hats instead of caps but they are a very good hat. the best of all they have a big feather in them & a brass bugle & eagle. we drawed shirts pants drawers shoes stockings & hats. we never have suffred yet for want of clothes. I am sorry to say we have lost our Capt. he applied for a furlough or a discharge & he got his discharge & is going to leave us. our 1st Lieut. comes in Capt (Jacob Paulk) he will make a good Capt but he is not as good drilled man as Rhoades. however I don't think we will have long to serve under any capt. the prisoners we have here says if we take Nashville they are gone & I think the next fight will be there. it will be all over by the time hot weather sets in. I am pleased with the idea of going south. I have wanted to go south for some time & this war is a good thing for a poor man for he can get to see the world & not cost him anything. I don't have an idea that the 39 will ever be in a fight. I think they will be held back as a reserve but if they do get in a fight they will show where they went for there is men in this Regt that will fight. well it is roll call & I will have to close for tonight.
Friday the 21st
I shall have to hurry & finish my letter for I expect we will have to leave this afternoon. our Capt is going to draw our R.R. money & I am going to have him put mine in an envelope that I backed to you & have him send it home. I don't think it will be very much, not over $8.00. I would have him

send it to me but we will be gone before it could get here & it might get lost so I thought I would have it sent home & if you need it you can use it & if I run out of money before we are paid off again I will have you send me some of it. they have had a fight in Ky a few days ago & our men whiped them. the rebbels will have to knuckle down before long. well I don't know what to write so I will close. Direct to Benton till I give you other directions.

    My love to you all.

    From your soldier boy Geo W

      To his Mother

                      Wilderness Camp in the Commerce MO

                                  Feb 25/1862

Dear Mother,

I seat myself in a pile of blankets with pen in hand to write you a few lines to let you know that I am still in good health & hope these few lines may find you all the same. We left Benton the next day after I wrote my last letter for Nashville & got down here to Commerce & we was ordered to stop here. We got off the boat & marched out about two miles & camped in the woods. They are getting up a brigade here to march through to New Madrid. It is about 40 miles from here by land. You look on the map of Mo & you will see it about 60 miles below Columbus. I expect we will be there some time. We are going there to cut of the retreat of the rebels. To keep them from going any further south. If we get down there I don't expect you will hear from me very soon for the mail cant get down there now. Not till we get Columbus. I don't want you to feel uneasy about me if you don't hear from me often for I shall take the best care of myself. You may not hear from me for 6 or 8 weeks but you must not feel uneasy. I would feel bad if I knew you was uneasy about me when I was well and you not know it.

I think they are leaving Columbus for our men have been down there for the last two days fireing at them & got no answer. They offered to give up Nashville providing we would not violate any private property. But our men would not accept it for they have property there that did not belong to them. I don't think they will stand much more fighting. Our Col says that we will *all be at home to celebrate the 4ᵗʰ of July. When we got here we found the 63d Ohio Regt here & there was lots of boys in it that I knew. There was 3 or 4 boys in it that Arthur & I had to work for us with the mill. They say the 18ᵗʰ & the 53d Ohio Regts are coming here. Harvey Pierce is in the 53d. I know several boys in both Regts. There is going to be a (???) brigade of 42 thousand leaves here next Sunday. Well Mother this is not much of a letter but I have such a poor place to write that I cant make much headway at writing. You can tell that by my writing. You need not write any more until you hear from me again for I will not get it. Well I don't know that I have any more to write so I will give you all good bye.*

From your Soldier Boy, Geo.

S.R. Church

PS The 18ᵗʰ Ills Regt was in the battle at Fort Donelson. I have not heard from Will for some time.

In the field New Madrid
March 15 1862

Dear Mother,

I take this opportunity of answering your letters which I received a few days ago but could not answer them on account of our position, We have been here almost two weeks. Camped within 3 miles of the enemy. Every few days we would go down to the fort & fire a few rounds at them just to let them know that we was here. The first day we came here we marched right down to the town. I was for going in but the secesh was so awful sassy & impudent about it as to bring up their gun boats & throw bomb shells at us & we had to retreat. The shell & shot flew thick over our heads but we all laid flat on the ground. We only got one man killed. We retreated back & camped. We did not do much more until yesterday & old Pope thought it was time he was doing something. So the night before the battle we went down & planted some batteries & by day light we was at them. That whole day you could hear nothing but cannons. At dark the firing ceased & by daylight the next morning what do you think. Not but one man in the fort & he was sound asleep. The infernal cowards had left. They run off & left their pickets out. We got them. We got 18 or 20 guns & any amount of ammunition & provision. Not one man in the 63 & 39 hurt. If that aint a miracle then I don't know what is. They cut the top off the trees over our heads & down amongst our heads & not one hurt. The reporter leaves here this morning for Cinti & he will take our letters through & he leaves in a few minutes so I will have to close. I just wrote to let you know that not a hair of me is hurt & I am well. You will hear from me soon again. Good bye GW

SC

PS Aust & Sam is well. Direct to Benton.

Near New Madrid
March 17, 1862

Dear Mother,
As I had not time to write much in my other letter I shall now give you a full account of our little knock down. As I said before the day we came in we was going to take the place right off but when we got most to the town we found that we had run on the wrong track for as soon as we got in range of their gun boats they let out on us. The balls & shells flew thick & fast for a while. We stood out in an open field with our colors flying. The nicest kind of a march to shoot at. They give us orders to lay flat on the ground. You better hope I laid close to the ground. I was not much thicker than a shingle when one of them shells would burst. We found we could not take the place as long as the gun boats was there & we had no large cannon with us so we retreated back & camped. All we was sent here for was to cut off their retreat & to keep their gun boats here while our men took Columbus & Island No 10. That is 10 miles above here & there is a place 10 miles below here called Pt. Pleasant the rebels had in their possession. From Pt. Pleasant to No 10 is 20 miles by water & only five by land. Their object in fortifying No 10 was to have their transportation at Pt. Pleasant & if they got defeated at No 10 they could cut across to the Pt & get on boats & leave before our gun boats could get around. But if they aint badly fooled I will treat for we have a battery planted at Pt. Pleasant & we have got New Madrid & good fortifications here & a large land force here & our gun boats are above them & a large land force

on the other side of the river. If they haint got their foot in it then I'll treat. The gun boats have been thundering away at them every since yesterday morning. Commander Foote has got some morters on his boats that throws a 225 lb shell. When one of them guns goes off they make a noise equal to thunder. Such cannoding as that is all we have heard for the last two days. I have always heard folks say that the secesh was cowards & would run. Now I know it. We shelled them one day from daylight till sun down & the next morning where do you think the secesh was. Well I don't know but they weren't here. They left one fellow asleep & left their pickets on guard. We got several large guns & any amount of ammunition. Pope estimated the value of the things we got at one million of dollars, Pretty good haul. We may be here some time yet & we may not be here but a little while. I don't know where we will go but expect we will go south. Likely to Memphis. I have not heard from Will since we was at Palmyra. They say they don't allow the soldiers to write letters in Ky. I got a letter from Adaline Dudrey (?) the other day & she said that she heard that Will had got a discharge & gone home. Well I must close. Tell the girls I have not time to write to them this time. I am in good health at present & hope this will find you the same. Write often & direct to St. Louis for I will get it as soon. No more at present.

From your soldier boy
Geo W. Waterman
S Church

New Madrid. Mo. Sunday April 6th/62

My Dear Mother,
I expect you will think it is time you was hearing from me again. well I am in good health at present & hope these few lines may find you all the same. I got two letters from home the 12th of last month & and that is the last I have heard from home. I expect it is on account of the high water came very near driving the rebels off of island no 10. One of our gunboats ran the blockade at no 10 last night before last. Yesterday about noon we got marching orders for some place unknown to all but the officers. We was ordered to have three days rations cooked by five oclock. We got all ready to

go by the time set but when five oclock came and then the order was countermanded. That is the way with a soldier he don't know one hour what he will do the next. I think we was going over the river to cut off the retreat of the rebels from no 10 but I don't know where we was going and don't know as we will go at all now. The rebels are getting all the force they can at Corinth Miss. There is going to be a hard battle there. If we get no 10 and Corinth I would not wonder if it would about wind this thing up. We are shure of no 10 but there is going to be a hard fight at Corinth unless we get more troops there. We hear heavy firing at No 10 and Point Pleasant every day. Some of the boys are beting all the time. some of the boys bet we will be at home in two months. Some in there and some of them says that they will bet that when we leave here we will start home. The prospect is very encouraging now.

The most of the boys heard from their money that Capt. Rhodes drawd for us. Some of them got more than they thought they would. Some got $20.00. If I got $8 I will be more than satisfied. If you have got the money I wish you would get 50 cents worth of postage stamps and send them to me for it is hard to get them here.

The boys are cutting up so that they have broke my chain of thought. Well I have just come back from meeting so now I will try & finish my letter. I wish our chaplain was here for I like to hear him preach better than any preacher I ever heard, I think of Little Freddy every day. When you wrote last you said that he was not very well.

I hope he won't be sick. How I would like to see the little fellow & the rest of you. I hope it won't be long till I can. Well Mother I was on guard last night so I don't feel much like writing, so I will close. Write as often as you can all of you. I don't have as much time as last winter for we drill all the time only Sundays. Tell Hudsons folks that ? and Sam was well the last time I saw them. They say they like the soldiers life the best kind. If you take the Cinti paper you will hear what is going on down here all the time. well I must close. My love to you all from your soldier boy Geo. W. Waterman

S.R. Church

New Madrid Mo. April 11th 1862

Dear Mother,
I received your letter dated 25th last Sunday. I had just put one in the office
about two hours before the mail comes in. I was glad to hear from home for
it has been some time since I had a letter from home. You will hear no
doubt before this reaches you of the glorious victory we have gained here at
No 10. I wrote in my last letter that we had marching orders but was
countermanded. That was Saturday. Monday morning we received
marching orders again with three days rations. We left here about 8 oclock
but it was 3 oclock before we got over the river. The rebbels had two
batteries planted on the opposite side of the river but when the old
Carondelet got down here they soon dried up. We landed on the other side
of the river a little below here and marched down opposite Point Pleasant
to camp or will lay down on the ground not having any tents. We was not
allowed to have the last bit of fire for we was giving it on the sly. We heard
that they was leaving No 10 and there was only one way for them to get
away and that place was where we was marching for as fast as possible.
They had their transport boats at Tipton intending to retreat from No 10
and get on the boats & put off but when their boats got up there they
found two of our snapping turtles anchored out on the river. There they was
we had them on every side. They could not march any further down than
Tipton for the swamps. They could not get their transport boats up for our
gun boats. we had troops between them at No 10 and then at Tipton. We
had five or six thousand of the larkins pened in as nice as pin. They had
to come under. We got three generals five thousand prisoners at least got all
their guns ammunition boats & every thing they had only what they
destroyed. Where has there been such a victory as that was and not a life
lost on either side. Pope is bound to get his name up now. You have seen
Pope. He is the man that came from Washington and married Horton's
daughter. We are now waiting for transportation to go to Fort Pillow near
Randolf. All the boats have gone up the Tennessee River after the sick &
wounded. They have had a hard battle at Corinth. The report is that
Grant got drove back and paid of his men taken prisoners. The prisoners
that we took here says that they will fight as long as their men held Corinth
& if we got that place they was gone up. One of the secesh Capts says that

he would take one of our gun boats and run it to New Orleans in spite of all the boats they had. The most of the prisoners was glad that they was taken. One of the capt said that he was better pleased than he had been for some time. They was the same men that we fought at New Madrid . They said that they knew they was whiped and there was no use of fighting. They can't fight anymore with a good heart. One of the prisoners wanted to know if there was any cherries up north now. They will be handed to him through the ten of diamonds. They are going to take the prisoners to Columbus Ohio but I don't know what Regt will go with them. I hope it will be the 39*th*. A fellow came from the 63*rd* Regt the other day & introduced himself to me. I know I had seen him but could not think who he was. I expect most is acquainted with him. His name is Bridgeman. He is orderly sargent of Co F the same Co. that Hudson's boys are in.

You got a very straight story of the fight at New Madrid. There was about 50 killed and wounded. The reason that I did not write sooner when we first came here was I did not want to write until after the fight for I knew you would be uneasy if you knew we was expecting a fight. I feel very much encouraged now the way things are working. I think it won't be long till we will take an up river passage. Won't that be a happy set of boys. We had a good deal of fun reading secesh letters at no 10. I am going to send this letter in a secesh envelope. We got a lot of them at No 10. I was glad to hear that you had received my money. There was more of it than I expected to get. Well I don't know that I have any more to write so I will close by stating that I am in good health and hope this may find you all the same. Write as often as you can all of you for I don't get much time to write. We drill all the good weather. From your son G.W. S. Church

PS Did you notice the temperance pledge that I sent to the telegraph

----

Fullersburg, Mississippi
*Apr 18*th *62*

Dear Mother,

I take this opportunity of answering your letter which I received in due time & was glad to hear from you. I am in good health at present & I hope this will find you all in like circumstances.

I thought the other day we were going to leave here for good but we did not go far & came back the same day. We have some sharp shooters at Glendale about 8 miles east of here & they were attacked last Thursday & we were called on to reinforce them but we had not got half way there when we heard that our men had repulsed the rebels so we came back. Genl Dodge left here the other day on an expedition unknown to us, but I think he is going to cooperate with Burnsides. There is not many troops here now. Col Fuller (our brigade commander) is in command of the brigade. We have a good deal of guard duty to do now since so many troops left – but that is easier than marching. I would not wonder if we were called off before long but I hardly think we will as long as Col Fuller is in command. I tell you Mother I feel very much encouraged now about the war. I honestly believe that this Springs campaign will wind it up. Every thing speaks in our favor. I see by the papers that Slidel (the southern minister) informs the south that they need not depend on any foreign help & advises them to work themselves back into the Union the best way they can. I think they will soon sneak back. I see there is a general movement now & I hope we will meet with success. I have but little confidence in Genl Grant. The papers says that in the course of three or four hundred years Grant is going to send some gunboats up to Vicksburg to see if the people haven't died of old age.

It is the opinion here now that Charleston will soon be ours. We don't hear much from the east lately. I don't believe there is much going on there.

I hope Pa can get some good job if the rolling mill starts, it will make good times there if they start it. The paymaster is here & we will soon draw our rations of green backs. The troops are in good health & fine spirits now. I never knew as little sickness in camp before, all hearty & fat. I weigh 143 lbs. now & when I left home my common weight was 125 & 28 lbs the most of the boys are fat as hogs.

Well I have nothing more to write so I will close for this time. You must excuse my poor writing this time for I have been to work about a week so I cant half write & this is miserable ink. No more at present but remain your loving son.

Geo Waterman
SC

Hamburg, Ten
Apr 23d/ 62

Dear Mother,
I now seat myself to write you a few lines to let you know that I am well
& hope these few lines may find you all the same.
I received your letter of the 3d at Cairo. a few days after I wrote to Mat we
left Oceola for Pittsburgh. After a long but pleasant trip we arrived safe.
We are a short distance above Pittsburgh landing. I don't know how long
we will stay here but I don't think we will march for a day or two. I
thought I had seen men before but this place beats all. Nothing but troops
for 20 miles around. I hope I can get to see the 18th Ills & the 18 Ohio. I
am glad that Halleck is to take command here for Grant is not a very good
general. I think this will be the decisive battle for the rebels are getting all
their force here & if we whip them out which we will they are gone up. We
left Commander Foot at Fort Pillow & we heard that he has taken the
place. We cant hear any news about what is going on here for every thing is
kept close. I expect we have near two hundred thousand men here & if the
rebels dont run they will get whipped shure. I expect our advance troops are
not far from the rebels & the fight may commence any day. We are on the
extreme left & clear back to the river. It would be some time before we
could get up. It will be a day or two before we can get ready to march.
I don't want you to feel uneasy about me if you dont hear from me very
often for I have no time to write. I am writing on my knee this time. Tell
Rhoda I was going to answer her letter this time but I have not time now
for we have to get things picked up. Tell little Fred that I hope he will see
me coming home before long & not be disappointed as he was before. Well
Mother I will have no time to write. Direct to Cairo. Write often.
Good bye
Geo Waterman
S. Church

30

Camp in the Woods Near Corinth, Miss
May the 3d 62

Dear Mother
Your letter of the 18ᵗʰ came safe to hand & I am very glad to hear from
home & know that you was all well. I don't get much time to write or I
would have answered your letter sooner. we are now camped within 10 miles
of Corinth but not much prospect of a fight yet. we still keep advancing
slowly but what is going on or what is going to be done I don't know for we
never hear anything that is going on. a good many think that we will not
have much of a fight here. there is a good deal of talk of the rebels
evacuating this place & go to Jackson or Memphis but I hope they will
stand battle here if they intend to fight at all for I have got tired of
following them up.
we are confident of success here & I long for the battle to come & have it
over with for I have an idea that all that comes out of this battle will have
the pleasure of soon returning home & I hope I will be one of the happy
ones. I don't think they will stand us much of a battle here for they are
coming in & giving themselves up nearly every day. they say that a good
many of their mens time is out & they refuse to enlist again.
I like the position that we are in & the commanders that we are under. we
are on the left of the army & in Popes command & in Tylers division. If
you hear of the battle before you get another letter from me you will know
what part of the engagement we was in if there should be one.
I have not heard from Will yet but they say the 18ᵗʰ is here. We are not
allowed to leave our Regt very far or I would try & find it.
them stamps came safe & I was very glad to get them. the paper that you
sent I never got. they have got the mail line blockaded so we cant get no late
news. I think they don't allow any papers to come to the soldiers. it takes
about three weeks for a letter to come through.
I have hard work to keep them stamps for all of the boys are out & as
soon as they hear of any of us geting stamps they all want to buy. I sold
some for five cent apiece.
We heard the other day the New Orleans was taken. I hope it is so but we
don't know for certain.

I want to write some to Mat & I have not much time so I will bring my letter to a close. write as often as you can & don't wait for me for I don't have much time to write.

Kiss little Freddy for me. Good bye for the present, from your son. G W W

S R C

Camp near Corinth, Mi
12th/62

Dear Mother.

Your letter of the 28th came safe to hand on the 10 of this month & I was glad to hear that you were all well. I am well at present & hope these few lines may find you all the same.

We are still camped in the same place we was when I wrote before. The rebels undertook to drive us out of our nest the other day but they was met with such a warm reception that they retreated back. The right & left wing of our army is working around slowly & if they don't attack us soon we will have them surrounded. I suppose you have head of the evacuation of Yorktown. That is the way they work. Whenever we expect the hardest battle they will evacuate, I would not wonder if about the time we got ready to fight them here they would be gone. If they stand us a fight here it will be the last hard fight we will have. The taking of New Orleans is a dampyner on them. I saw a piece in the paper that Jeff Davis's wife thought the southern confederacy about played out. I think so too. A prisoner that they took at Yorktown said that we had Yorktown but we had not got No 10 & Fort Donelson yet. If the rebels knew what we have done lately they would not fight any more. I am in a hurry for this battle to come off for I think we will see better times after this. I suppose we have more artillery in the field before here than was ever in one place before. It will be a regular artillery fight. We have larger cannon here than was ever in a field fight before.

After the battle here I shall try & find Will if nothing happens to prevent. We aint allowed to leave our Regimental lines while near the enemy. I should like the best kind to see him. I got a letter from Lewis the same time I got yours.

Well I must close as I want to answer Mattie's letter. Write as often as you can all of you. If Pa is in Ills when I come through I am going to stop there. I shall try and keep well & hope to soon see home safe & sound. Tell Fred that I hope to see him soon. Good bye for the present.

From your son, Geo Waterman
S Church

P S I was going to write some to Mat but I cant now but will write soon. Tell her not to wait for me but write as often as she can.

Farmington, Mississippi
May 26th 1862

Dear Mother,

As I have a few leisure hours to myself I thought I could spend them no better than writing you a few lines for I know it is a pleasure to you to hear from me & I like to hear from home. I received your letter of the 1st last evening. I was glad to hear that Pa had got home. You did not say whether the folks was well or not, but I suppose they was or you would have mentioned it.

I am enjoying good health at present & hope these few lines may find you all the same. That disease you spoke about is very common among the soldiers here but somehow I aint troubled with it. I think I had ought to be thankfull for the good health I have been blest with since I have been in the army. Sometimes I feel a little unwell but I never give up as long as I can help it for I know how I feel when I am sick & away from home. If I get sick so that I will not be fit for duty I am going to try & get a furlough. Several boys in our camp are home on sick furloughs. There aint as much sickness in our camp now as there was when we first come here. I did not feel very well while we were on the boat but as soon as we got off I felt as well as ever.

Tho Hudson was over to our camp this morning. He was taken prisoner at Athens Ala. They let him off on guard of honor & not to take up arms against them until regularly exchanged. He says he has seen both sides of the picture now. He said he was not treated very well. He said they had not half enough to eat & that all the houses in Corinth was VA Hospitals.

79

He says they are dieing off like sheep & a good many of them are sick of fighting & want to get out of it. A good many of them are handcuffed for trying to desert. A good many of them thinks they hold Fort Donelson & No 10 yet & that they are about to whip us out.

I cant find out much of anything that is going on here. Every thing has been quiet for several days & it is hard to find out anything that is going on. I think very likely we will be here for sometime yet.

If this battle don't come off till our men gets Memphis they are gone up for that is their only chance of escape.

I see by the papers that McClellan is beginning to wake them up a little & I think it is about time he was doing something.

If there is a good wheat & corn crop in Ill I would not wonder if Pa would do well to have a grist mill attached to the saw mill if he could get one cheap. If I get out of the army safe I would like to run it for I don't know what I will go at when I get home.

You spoke about using some of my money to buy flowers with. That is all right. If I had been there I would have given it freely. Keep them to remember me by. Well I will have to go on guard before long so I will bring my letter to an end.

Send me 50cts worth of stamps if you can get them. Write as often as convenient. My love to you all. From your son.

Geo Waterman
S Church

Tell the girls to write as often as they can.

Letter # 44

Camp near Boonville Mississippi
June 8th/62

Dear Mother

Your letter of the 25th came safe to hand on the 5th of this month & I embrace this the earliest opportunity of answering it. I am well at present & hope this may find you all the same.

I suppose you have heard before this time of the evacuation of Corinth. We got orders on the 27th to have 3 days rations cooked & to be ready to move at a moments time. On the 28th we made a move toward the enemy. Drove in their pickets & got within range of their guns & opened fire on them about 9 oclock & continued until dark without much loss on our side. We buried 30 of their dead the first day & how many they took away we don't know. On the night of the 28 we dug trenches & planted 2 of our siege guns & about daylight we upended a few of their batteries for them. Nothing much but artillery fighting the 29. We was all out once on the 29 to charge on one of their batteries but the order was countermanded before we went far & I was glad of it at the time but have wished since that we had went & took it for they have negroes to work the battery while they was getting ready to leave. There was five wounded in our Regt, two of our company. About 10 oclock the night of the 29th the cars came in & such cheering & yelling was never heard before as them butter nuts made. It commenced on the sight of their lines & went the whole length. We all thought they was getting some reinforcements what made them cheer. At daylight on the 30 we saw a black smoke in Corinth which we took at first to be the cars but it come thicker & blacker & in a little while there was one of the awfullest explosions I ever heard. We all come to the conclusion they had left & blowed up their magazine. In a few minutes our Regt was ordered out to skirmish through the woods to try & find out what that explosion was. Our Major told the General that if he was not stoped he was going in to Corinth & shure enough we did go in & planted the first flag on the court house.

We are now camped in the woods between the Memphis & Charlston RR & the Mobile & Ohio. How long we will stay here or where we will go when we leave here is more than I can tell & if any man can tell where the secesh is they can do more than I can. I don't think they will ever get their army together again. If they do I don't see where they will make a stand. To look at the thing right I think the Southern Confederacy about played out. I hope it wont be long till we can all go home. I got a letter from Will a few days ago & answered it today. He was well when he wrote. I was so glad to hear that the Murdock boys got caught. The way they did I would like to have seen them.

Well I shall have to stop. I will write again as soon as I have time & a better place. If you don't hear from me often don't think me sick for the way we are fixed I cant write often. The RR is all destroyed & it is 55 *miles to the river so we don't get mail very often. Tell Mat I have not time to answer her letter. Write often as you can all of you. My love to you all. Good Bye.*

Your son Geo Waterman
S R Church

Camp five miles South of
on the Tuscumbia River
June 12/62

Dear Mother.

This pleasant afternoon finds me seated in the shade of a tree trying to write you a few lines to let you know that I am still enjoying good health & hope this will find you all the same.

Since I wrote to you last we have moved 20 miles back toward Corinth. We could not stay there on account of water. The creeks were all drying up & we dug for water but could not get any so we had to strike out. We are now camped on a nice stream of water. I expect we will be here some time unless our brigade is stationed at some place for the summer. There is talk now that our brigade will be stationed at Memphis or Florence, Ala. I am glad we don't have to march down south this hot weather. We would lose half our army if we did. We heard yesterday that the Mississippi river was opened the whole length now. They are repairing the RR that runs to Memphis & will soon have it ready for use. If we are stationed at Memphis we will be apt to go there soon & then I will try & get a furlough. I intend to try & get leave of absence & go to see Will & the rest of the Pomeroy boys.

You said you hoped I could be home to celebrate the fourth of July. Indeed I would like to but I am afraid I will not. I think that the western division has got about done fighting & will now lay by & let the Eastern division do something. I think it will be sometime yet before we can go home but our fighting is about done & we will see better times.

I received your letter that had them stamps in & was glad to get them for I had just put my last stamp on the last letter I wrote to you. I suppose you have seen the account of the evacuation of Corinth so I will not say anything about it any more than it was good for our hides that we did not have to fight for it. If we had 50,000 men inside of such fortifications the whole southern confederacy could not whip us. Well I must stop for I want to write some to Mattie yet to night. I have a poor chance to write but I shall try to write as often as I can & you must all do the same.

My love to you all

Your son Geo Waterman

S C

June 21, 1862

Since I wrote this other letter I have received one from you & as I have a chance of sending it in a few days I thought I would write a few more lines to send with it.

Our Lieut is going home with his father & if they go by the river they can drop this in the office of the boat stop there & if not they can put it in the office at Hocking Port.

There appears to be quite an excitement at present about England & France. A good many think they will give us a (banter?). There is a good many going in the Regular servis. Several in this Regt is & some of our Company is going. I know of one in Co K that will not go. For my part I have no fears of England & France and have no desire to join the Regulars.

Well I have no news to write so I will close by stating that I am in excellent health & hope this may find you all the same. No more this time.

Your son

Geo Waterman

S.R.C.

Camp Clear Creek, Miss

July 6th/62

Dear Mother,

This pleasant evening finds me seated before our writing desk trying to write you a few lines to let you know that I am still alive well & hearty & hope this mat find you all the same. I have had most excellent health this summer & hope it may continue so.

I was glad to hear you had a good visit in the country. I am afraid by the way the family is going to scatter out you will be lonesome. Oh how I would like to be at home about a month this summer to spend the hot weather. I can stand it very well while we are laying around in camp but if we go on a march it will go hard with a good many of us. I don't know how it would go with me & only hope we wont have the trial of it but I would not wonder if we left here before long for we had orders this morning to cook two days rations & be ready to march at any time. But we may not go for we have had several orders like that lately & did not march.

I suppose there was a picnic or a celebration or something of the kind going on there the fourth. I would like to have been there to take part in it but circumstance would not admit of it. Perhaps you will wonder what was going on in camp. Well all that was done distinguish it from any other day was this, we were exempt from all duty & at noon every battery had to fire the National salute. You could hear every cannon in every direction that day.

There is quite an excitement now about Richmond. Some fears that McClellan will get whipped out there. Never has there been a time that I waited with so much anxiety the coming events as at the present nor been so anxious for our men to gain a victory at Richmond. Things will look discouraging to me if we get defeated there. But I cant help but think we will come out victorious.

I see by the papers that the President has been to see Scott & get his advice for the best way of bringing this war to a speedy close & I hope they will soon accomplish it. Our good General has been taken from us & a higher position assigned him. He is next to McClellan now 2d in command. Success to him where ever he may be.

Our Col bid us farewell the fourth, after dress parade he made us a short speech & told us that he was going to leave us & hoped we would keep our good name. He said he might do us as much good away from us as he could with us & if he could we might rest assured he would do all he could for us. I was sorry to have him leave us for he has been a father to this Regt. I cant see why so many officers are resigning. I am afraid they think we will be kept in the servis some time yet but I hope not. Still I don't think we will be discharged before fall if we are then.

In my last letter to Uncle Zeb I told him to tell me where Uncle Reuben was & I would write to him but I think I wont now. I might get an answer & I might not & I have as many correspondents as I want to write to.

I am glad to know that Saml Jennings speaks well of me at home, I don't think there is one in the Co that can say any harm of me. I try to do what is right by every one & do my duty to the best of my ability. Saml is a nice young man & very good company. He is in the same mess with me. We have a good civil set of boys in our tent. They call us the missionary squad because we are singing nearly all the time & are a civil set of boys.

I think you will have a good time when you get to washing my overcoat. If we have to spend another winter in the servis I shall send for my over coat. So if you have time I wish you would put a pocket in each side of it. Have the top of the pocket about even with the bottom of the cape so my belt will come below my pocket.

That old coat has done me more good servis than any coat I ever had. It was most to long & I took my knife & cut some off.

Mat writes that Pa is going to Ill again. If they put up a mill out there write how they got along with it. I should like very much to be there to run it. If Pa is there when we get discharged I shall stop there.

Is there any talk there about any foreign nation aiding the South? A good many thinks that Eng will acknowledge the southern confederacy. If England does the north will have to make war with England & the south. But I hope nothing of the kind will happen. If we come off victorious at Richmond I think it wont be long till this fuss is settled. We can soon tell how things will turn for the fighting has commenced at Richmond & McClellan wont allow anything to be published till it is all over. Well I have wrote about all I can think of so I will bring my letter to an end. If I am not mistaken today is Freddys birth day. How many times I have thought of him.

Write as often as convenient. No more at present, From your son, Geo W.

S.C.

85

Camp Clear Creek, Mississippi
July 15/62

My dear Mother:

I now seat myself to answer your ever welcome letter which came safe to hand last evening. I was glad to hear you were all well. I am still in good health & hope this will find you all the same.

I received a letter from Lewis Aunt Jane & Mattie last evening.

I was glad to hear that my money went through safe. You said you had taken 2 ½ out of the other but will replace it. You need not mind replacing but keep yourself in stamps & send me some along as I need them till we get where I can get some. I can get them here sometimes by paying five cts apiece for them.

We are to be inspected this morning by Halleck's Agt General. We have to have everything in nice order. There has been a hard battle at Richmond. A good many lives lost on both sides but the most on the rebble side.

McClellan retreated 17 miles & fought on the retreat. It was done in good order & shows good Generalship. He had not force enough to hold his position so he fell back & is now reinforced by Burnside's whole army & will soon try them again. A good many thinks by the time he gets ready to fight them again they will be gone. I hope not for it only lengthens the war every time they evacuate. They wont fight us any more unless they have three times our number.

I hope they will stand & give McClellan fight when he gets ready again. He will whip them so bad they wont know themselves.

I think it is strange Will did not get my letter. I know I directed it right. I wish he could get leave of absence & come & see me. There is no chance of getting a furlough now.

One year ago today I (very Patroticaly) went up to Cutter Station & enlisted but I aint half as Patriotic now as I was then. I will see my country is a worse condition than it was then before I will enlist again, but don't think me homesick, not so. I have commenced to help put this rebellion down & I will see the end of it if I live that long & then I will bid the army good bye & I aint the only one in that fix & when I take another oath I will understand the nature of it before I take it.

Well I don't know of any news to write so I will close. Write as often as *convenient.*

Your son
Geo Waterman
S R Church

Camp Clear Creek, Miss
July 27/62

Dear Mother
The mail has just come in and I got your letter of the 18th. I have been looking for it for several days but did not get one as it had been over a week since I have written to you. I had just got ready to write when the mail came in. I am still in good health and hope this may find you all the same. I don't know that I ever had any better health in my life than I have had since I have been in the service.

You write that it was very hot weather there now. I expect it is as hot there now as it is here. It seems that we have had our hot weather here sooner than in Ohio for it is cooler now than some time ago. The thermometer has been as high as 130 degrees in the shade. There is not as much sickness now as there was some weeks ago. W. Cole has been sick about four weeks He has the typhoid fever but is getting better now.

It seems hard for a person to tell what is going to be done. I try to believe that it won't be long till this war will end but sometimes I think and painful is the thought that it will be sometime yet before I will have the pleasure of returning home. Things looked more favorable before the fight at Richmond than it does now. It seems that our retreat from Richmond caused them to take fresh courage. The President has called for 200,000 more men. I see in the last paper that 180,000 had been raised. That is the way I like to see them turn out. I think it is the intention to put down this rebellion as soon as possible. Jeff Davis is trying to get England to acknowledge the Southern Confederacy but he is making slow progress at it. I don't think we will have much more fighting to do unless we go east and I don't think we will.

I should like very much to go home awhile but as I can't I will have to content myself the best I can till I can go home. I have with my own free will got in it. I shall try and do my duty to the best of my ability and take things as patient as I can till I get my foot out of this trap.

We have drawed new guns and in my opinion we won't get discharged for some time yet. We have very nice guns now much better than the muskets. There is no prospect of leaving here soon and as for work we have none. We are the best of times now. Send me a paper once in awhile for I think they will come through now. Well I will have to close for the present so no more.

Your son Geo. W.
S.R.C.

Camp Clear Creek, Miss
Aug 7/62

Dear Mother,

I now seat myself to answer your letter which I received in due time. I was glad to hear that you were all well. I am enjoying excellent health at present & hope this may find you all the same.

You wrote that there was quite an excitement around there about the Guerrillas. There is any amount of them around the border states & they are a curse to the country. there had not ought to be any quarter shown them when they are caught. there is little talk of us going to Ky but I think it is all talk. some of the boys say they heard the Col. say we was going to Ky. how I wish they would put this Regt in there after old Morgan. we would soon have him as shy of us as Jeff Tompson was at New Madrid. I believe I have never told of him yet. while we were marching from Commerce to Madrid we run on to old Jeff Tompson & captured some of his men & cannon but he made tracks for New Madrid as fast as his horse could carry him. some of the negroes said that when he got there he had no hat nor sword & told that the 39th Ohio was coming & the men was all six ft high & could jump 20 ft. one of his men that we took at no 10 asked a fellow in our Co if he belonged to the 39th. he told him he did. then the prisoner told him he was six ft & went on to say what Thompson had said. quite a compliment.

I don't doubt but there is traitors in Pomeroy & they ought to be watched. I *would like to be there to keep an eye on them. I wont advise anyone to spit secesh in my face if I ever get off this show. if they do they will do it at their own risk. I have went through a little too much to stand & hear any one sympathize with the south.*

we don't hear anything from Jim Richmond lately. I don't believe they will have another fight there if they can help it. I would not wonder if they evacuated Richmond. they will if they can but they have got a General among them. now that will make them look wild.

the Government is taken a step now that will wind the thing up. that is the confiscation of rebble property even the negroes. if that will end the war I say go in on it. some of the Northern Democrats say we are fighting to free the negroes. it will put an end to slavery. that is true but if we cant have Union & slavery let us have the Union without the slavery. I dont like to have the name of fighting to free the negroes which will be throwed up to us. but now I am in it & cant help it I don't care what way they take to bring this war to an end. some says the south cant hold out much longer. the way we have been going they will hold out longer than we will. wherever they go they make a mark. how is it with us. when we go in their country we guard their property & are not allowed to touch a single thing. we leave their negroes unmolested on their plantations to raise their crops for them while they are out fighting against us & if we come to a family that is so unfortunate as not to have any negroes to work their farms & the men are off fighting against us. that family is kept by our Government. I think things will take a turn before long for it seems that the North are geting waked up to a sense of their duty & I hope they will go to work in earnest & bring this war to a speedy end. it is discouraging to men when they are willing to do a thing to be held back.

there is some talk of this brigade going to Corinth to stay there but I don't know.

we were paid off again yesterday but I dare not send much money in a letter for fear it wont get there if the mail is what it will be soon after pay day. likely I will send 5 dollars in my next letter & if it goes through safe I will try another. well I must bring my letter to a close. I was on guard last night & aint in very good trim for writing today. so no more this time.

Your son G Waterman

S R C

Camp Clear Creek, Miss.
Aug 10/62

Dear Mother.

Your letter of the 3d came safe to hand this morning & as to day is Sunday & we have nothing to do I have a good chance to write. I am in good health & hope this will find you all the same. One year ago today the brave Genl Lyon fell at the battle of Springfield & the batteries that were there are here now & they are going to have a grant celebration. I was glad to hear of them catching them two rebels in Pomeroy. There is rebels every where & they will have to watch them. I like to hear of traitors getting used the way them two was at Newburgh. That is the way to use them & then they will think we aint to be fooled with. I will hate it if the North has to draft to get all the soldiers we want but I believe they will do it if they don't enlist very fast. There is some that I would hate to see drafted & some that I would like to see. I am glad I aint laying around home now like some are doing nothing although I would like to be there at present as well as anybody but I would never stand a draft.

I am getting impatient for this war to come to an end! It seems to me as if they were not doing any thing at all. We are laying around in camp doing nothing & cant hear of anything being done. After the 11th of this month there is going to be a general muster & all absent from their Regt at that time (unless accounted for) will be considered deserters. I think there is going to be something done before long for they are getting all the men together & we are kept very close here now. We aint allowed to go from our Regt to another.

I was going to tell you to get that draft in your name for if it was in my name no person but me could draw it. I think I will send five dollars in this letter & if it gets through I will try another. I don't like to send much at a time. I will send five & if it don't get through it wont be much any how. Every battery within hearing is firing a salute for Lyon now at 12 oclock. I would like to be at home when Uncle Moses is there. I don't know why he don't write. I wrote to him last.

Well I have wrote all I can think of so I will close.

No more this time.
From your son
Geo Waterman
S.R. Church

Camp Clear Creek
*August 18, 1862 ***

Dear Mother,
Your letter of the 10th came safe to hand this morning & I hasten to
answer it for it may be the last chance I will have for some time for we
expect to leave here in a few days, we are going to move about 20 miles
from here on the Memphis & Charleston R.R. to guard the road. We will
be out in country where there is plenty of vegetables & the confiscation bill
has past and we are carrying the order to affect. Yesterday they took one
company out each regt in this brigade and two wagons from each regt and
went out in the country to get corn apples and peaches & they came back
pretty well loaded. That is the way I like to see the thing work, that looks
like doing something. I see by the papers that Pope's army are living entirely
on the enemy. Oh how the rebbels hate Pope. Pope and Seigle has given the
rebbels a nice thrashing in va. The war has commenced again and it has
commenced in earnest. It is believed that when they leave Richmond they
will try to take Corinth back but they will have a sweet time of it.
Mother I have been trying to get out of this Co. & get a better job if I
can. There is a fellow in the 63rd Regt that has a brother in law that is
kind of a R.R. & Telegraph agent and this fellow in the 63rd is going to
get a job with him and he thinks he can get me a job as fireman or engineer
on the cars. If he can it will suit me better & I will be making more than
I am here & will have an easier time. Won't have any marching or
standing guard to do. If I can get that job I will make from 20 to 25
dollars a month. I aint certain of it and have not said any thing about it
only to that fellow in the 63rd but he will do his best to get me a job. I am
getting tired of this thing and would like to have a change. It will be no
worse place for me either for bad company or danger for I am as much

exposed to both here as any where I could go but I am the same George that I was when I left home. You said you was afraid I did not fare well down here. we don't fare very well but better than folks at home think we do. A soldiers life is a hard life make the best of it but it aint as bad as it might be. We have plenty to eat such as it is. We are doing as well here now as we did when we were up north.

I sent 5 dollars in my last letter but I have no more to spare now or I would send some of this. I sent you a 2 dollar present the other day. I thought you would like a present of that kind as well as any thing else. It isn't as good as the one I got at Palmyra but it is as good as I could get. I had it taken in my shirt sleeves. Well I have no more time to write much more so I will close. Tell Freddy I have not time to write him a letter now but will write him one before long. No more this time. your son G.W.W. I am in good health and hope this will find you the same.

*Pension Letter # 1

Iuka Mississippi
Aug 24th 62

Dear Mother

I embrace this opportunity of writing you a few lines to let you know that I am well & hope this may find you all the same. we left our old camp on Clear Creek on the 20th & arrived at this place the 22d & we have been so busy every since that I have had no time to write. I have not much time to write now for I am on duty today but don't go to work till 5 oclock this evening. it is so warm that we don't do any thing in the heat of the day. we are cutting down timber about a mile around our camp to keep the enemy from coming in on us. we have a very nice camp here close to a beautifull little town. it is one of the fashionable towns of the south for the aristocracy of the south to spend the summer. there is some nice springs & Summer houses here & nice country, around here but their visitors is few this summer. two Co of our Regt is at Eastport on the Tenn river about 8 miles from here. it is hard to tell how long we will stay here. we are doing very well now for it is a good country for fruit & there is plenty of it here. we are under many obligations to Jeff Davis for advising the southern

92

people to plant corn instead of cotton. we happened down here in the right time to help them gather in their crops. the first night we camped when we was coming here we camped near a fellows house & some of the boys went there to get some water & he told them that the swamp water was good enough for the northern men & ordered them away but he made the thing worse. the boys got all the water they wanted & went & cleaned out their orchard & took every thing on the place that was good to eat. that is the way the Lincolnites treats them when they get too saucy.

the mail has just come in & I got a letter from you & Mat & a Telegraph. I did not get the other one but was very glad to get this one. I was glad that money went through safe. I cant spare any more now for I like to have some by me. I think we will get paid off again before long & then I will send some more. you wanted to know who our Col. is now. his name is Gilbert. he was Lieut Col. Tell Mat I have not time to write to her now but will write soon. tell Mis Sims that Geo is well & hearty. he is a first rate fellow & I like him. he calls me his Pomeroy friend. well will have to close for I will have to go to work soon. excuse my poor writing for I have a poor pen. send some stamps if you can get them. No more

Your Son Geo Waterman

S R C

Iuka, Mississippi
Sept 8/62

Dear Mother,

I received a letter from you last evening & I now seat myself to ans it. I don't expect to write much for I don't feel very well to day. I went to the doctor this morning & got excused from duty but I thought I could write if nothing els.

It was a hard trip on us going to Cherokee & back so soon & it was hot weather.

The news we get now aint very encouraging. I am afraid our men got the worst of it in the late battle in Virginia by what we hear. Sometimes I get almost discouraged at the way things is working. The prospect aint very bright now but things may take a turn before long & a good many thinks we are going to Ky but I think it is doubtful. I think I will write one more letter to Will & if he don't get it I will give it up. I thought he was at Memphis but I shall direct now to Jackson.

The day we went to Cherokee it was very hot & we did not get there till after dark so we did not pitch our tents but slept out & I caught cold & have not been very well since. I went & got some powders & an excuse from duty. I don't want you to feel uneasy about me for I aint sick but a little unwell.

I got that paper you sent to me & was very glad to have it. You need not send me any stamps at present for I can get plenty of them here.

There aint anything of importance going on here at present so it is dull times for writing. Tell Mat to write as often as she can & I will try to answer her letters.

Well I guess I will close. My love to you all.

Your son

Geo Waterman

S. Church

Camp Clear Creek Sept 14th/62

Dear Mother,

I now put myself down on the ground to write a few lines to let you know that I am still bobing around. You will see by the heading of my letter that we have got back to old Clear Creek. We are camped between our old camp & Corinth. We will not stay here long for we have not pitched our tents. I think very likely we will be ranting around for some time now. I would not wonder if we would go into Tenn or Ky for they are sending a good many troops in Ky.now. We may stop in Corinth. On Friday we got orders to cook 3 days rations and by 5 o'clock we had orders to strike tents. We soon broke up house keeping and had everything loaded and ready to start but did not leave until 4 in the morning. I wrote in my last letter that I was not very well. I am better now but the march went hard with me but I think I will come out all right yet. I feel kind of discouraged the things is going now. There is too much strife among our Generals to do any good. They is to proud to get along well and in my way of thinking they will not prosper *until they are humbled a little. I think according to scripture that the north will get whipped before they conquer and we are as near whipped now as we ever was. I wish the north would draft every man that is subject to a draft. That is the only way to get them out in time. The south is getting a start while we are waiting for more men.*

Well I hope things will take a turn before long.

Well I guess I will close. Excuse my poor writing if you would see the way I am writing you would not wonder at my poor writing but as it is my day to write I thought I would try it.. If I don't write regular now don't feel uneasy. I expect to get a letter from you when the mail comes in.

No more at this time, your son G.W. S.C.

I expect Matt will give me heck for not writing to her but I can't this time.

Corinth Mississippi
Sept 22/62

Dear Mother.

It has not been but a few days since I wrote to Mat but as I have plenty of time I thought I would write a few lines for I know you will be glad to hear from me.

I am still bobing around in camp but don't feel much like going with the Regt now I don't think I will as long as I can get to stay with the teams. I have marched & done duty when I did not feel like it & now I have made up my mind to stop it for I did not come out here to kill myself nor I don't intend to. I have a very easy time here laying around in camp & keep track of our Company traps. I haven't had a letter from you this week but expect it is in the office over in town but we cant get the mail without an order. We have very encouraging news now from the east. If things keeps on the way they are going now they will wind the thing up now soon. This is their last hard struggle & if they get defeated in every battle as we hear they do it will dampen their spirits a little. I thought that when our new troops got out things would take a turn & shure enough they have. The new troops comes in faster than we lose the men so our army aint running down any while we kill as many of them as they do of us & they have no more men to bring in the field. I do hope they will bring the thing to an end before winter for I don't want to spend another winter in the army.

We heard from our Regt this morning. They are still running old Price. They are 7 miles the other side of Iuka & pushing on after him. The 6th Minesota Regt run on our Regt (the 39th) some way & thought they was rebels & fired into them & wounded 4 or 5 of our boys returned the fire & killed 7 of them. They was not close enough to do much hurt. It may be some time before I will get with the Regt again if they run Price very far. I shall not go with them till I feel like marching if it aint for three years yet. If you see Ms. Simms tell her that George is well. He is in our Company teamster.

I think Price is trying to get into Tenn so as to make a junction with Bragg. If he does he will stand fight, but he must not forget that Buell is in there somewhere.

Well I don't know that I have any more to write so I will close, I will write every week when I have a chance but we are moving around a good deal lately. No more at this time.

Your loving son
Geo Waterman
SC

Corinth Mississippi
Sept 28th/62

Dear Mother,

I received your letter of the 14th last evening and was very glad to hear from you. I received a letter from Will last night. he was well when he wrote. I was very glad to hear from him.

I am here at Corinth yet with about 12 of our reg't. I feel better than I did when I wrote before but I don't intend to go to the regt until I feel like doing duty. we are considered convalessents, neither sick nor able for duty. If I had my descriptive roll with me I would have went to the General Hospital before this not because I am sick but because they are sending all the sick north. I can't get my descriptive roll till I go to the regt unless the capt sends it to me.

I think you have quite exciting times in Pomeroy now. I wish I was there.

every dog fights better at home you know; I wish this Ohio brigade was in va after old Jenkins we would learn him how to march the 39th & 27th Ohio regts can beat anything marching that ever left this state of Ohio. the day we left Iuka for Clear Creek two cos of our regt marched 35 miles and never complained. they are the most willing set of men I ever saw. I wish they would send us to western Va this winter. I suppose you have heard about the fight with Price before this so I will not write much about it. they have routed him and drove him off & I don't think he will be back soon again.

I don't think there is much rest for the troops now for awhile. they have cut the baggage down to a small amount to what it was. Only two tents allowed to a co and the officers ain't allowed to have their trunks with them & not over 80 lbs of baggage to haul. that looks to me as if they intend to do some marching it looks so much so to me that I don't intend to go with them till I feel like keeping my end up.

You say you can't help but feel a little uneasy about me. I expected you would but I don't want you to worry much about me for I am doing very well at present & just sick enough to not do duty. you will perhaps want to know what ails me. I have this chronic diarrhea. it is a common complaint and don't seem to hurt a fellow much only makes him weak. I believe if I should go to the Hospital that I would be sent north for two boys in our Co went to the hospital the other day & they are sent north now but I don't care where I am if I don't get worse.

well I don't know of any thing more to write so I will close. I will write every week while I am here but if I go to the regt I will not have a chance to write but don't feel uneasy.

your son Geo Waterman

Corinth, Mississippi
Oct 7/62

Dear Mother,
As I have a little more time to write I thought I would write a few lines to you. I am still gaining & am most well again. the way things is working here now is enough to make a sick man well anyhow. Price & his army is

about played out now & we still hear good news elsewhere. Things begin to look brighter than they did some time ago & I hope they will continue so till this rebellion is ended. you will likely hear of this battle before this reaches you & hear the particulars of it. likely if I undertook to describe it I would tell some things that was not so for I was not in the fight but saw a good part if it & was over the battle field yesterday & saw as much as I wanted to see, it is an awful sight. our wounded don't look half as bad as the rebels. I think we can live in peace for a while here now.

I got three of the telegraphs that you sent me.

I saw a rebel Col. that was killed & he wrote this inscription on a paper & pinned it to his sleeve.

(Col Johnson 20th Miss. this body will be left where discovered)   I suppose by that they intended to get a chance to take him off the field for they sent in a flag & truce to bury their dead but Rosecrans sent word back that he would bury the dead & for him to get out of there as soon as possible. I think he thought Rosecrans advice a good one & had better take it for it was not long after that he left. well it is getting late & I must stop. if things quiet down a little I will write a little more regular. dont feel uneasy if you don't hear from me once a month. no more at this time. Good night

Your son Georgie

S C

Kiss little Fred for me. every little boy I see I think of him.
you may send me a few stamps in the next letter if you can get them for I am about out & so is my chinck.

Corinth Mississippi
Oct 13th/62

Dear Mother,

I have just rec'd a letter from you & was very glad to hear that you was all well. I am about as well as common & am with the Regt. again. I went to the Regt two days after I wrote to you last. They was about 35 miles from here & I got out to them about two hours before they started back. I rode most of the way out & part of the way back. I think we will stay here a *while now.*

I was glad to get to my Co. again. It was the first time that I have been sepperated from my Co since I have been out & I hope it will be the last time. We got some of the largest & best sweet potatoes that I have ever eat in my life. When I was out to the Regt when we find anything good to eat we always take care of it. I saw James Weether this morning. He is in the 7th Kansas co. He has been sick for some time but is around now. He is as good at gassing as the rest of them. It is reported now that Bragg is going to make an attack on this place when he leaves Ky but I don't think he will have much to Bragg on by the time he gets as nice a licking as Price did. I wish they would whip out that little force on the Kanawha & not let them get so much salt. That is what they need the worst & that is what we ought to keep from them. I wish they would send us in there, we would show them how to make salt.

I am about as well as ever & think I will get along now. My feet is sore is about all ails me now. I expect we will be paid off soon now. We will get 52 dollars when we do get it. Four months pay due us the last of this month. I shall try to send 50 of it home. I sold my revolver so that will be all the spending money I will want. I shall send all the money home I can. Well I want to write a letter to Aunt Henrietta yet before the mail goes out so I will have to close this one. No more this time. My love to you all. Your son

Geo Waterman

S C

P.S. Geo Simms wants you to tell his mother if you see her that he is well. He says he don't hear from there very often. He is afraid they will be uneasy about him if they don't hear from him.

G W W

#57

Corinth, Mississippi
Oct 19/62

Dear Mother.

*I now seat myself to pen a few lines to you to let you know that I am well
& hope this may find you all the same. This is the day for me to get a letter
from you but the mail has not come in yet. I thought I would go to writing
till the mail did come in. It is all quiet here now and we have settled down
in side of the breast works east of Corinth but how long we will stay here
is hard to tell. One thing certain if we don't make a move before long we
wont make one this winter for it will be impossible to move artillery here in
the winter on account of the roads. I don't fancy the place here for it will be
so muddy in the winter & then we aint handy to water. We have to haul
water about one half a mile & not very good when we do get it. It is the
greatest wonder in the world that all shaking our toe nails off with the ague
now for it is the meanest weather here now I ever saw, hot enough in the
daytime to boil eggs in the sun & cold enough at night to freeze the horns
off a muley cow.*

*If you take the Cin Commercial you will hear all about the battle of
Corinth & the part the 39th took in it. The paper states that this is the
largest Regt in Grants army. Our Col has resigned & now Major Noyse
will come in Col. There aint many of the boys that likes him. He is too
strict to suit them. I expect we will be paid off the first of next month. If
you have the change I wish you would buy me a good gold pen & send in
the next letter. I have spent enough since I have been in the servis to buy me
two gold pens & then borrowed pens half of the time. I had a good one &
some of the boys broke it. I have a good holder & only want the pen. Get
a tolerable fine & limber pen. I have not the change to send now but will
send it when we get paid off. We have to pay three prices for anything here.
Only $15 for a pair of boots. Well I will close till the mail comes in.
Well the mail has come in & I did not get no letter from home but I got
one from Arthur's Brother. We have quite encouraging news now from Ky
& I am shure we gained the day here so I don't see but the tide is turning
in our favor. If they only do as well in Va. I think we would soon clean
them out. I hear there is an army getting ready to move up the Kanawha*

after salt & are going to pay for it with shot & shell. I hope they will succeed.

Well I don't know of any thing more to write so I will close. My love to you all.

Geo Waterman
S R Church

58th letter

Corinth, Mississippi
Sunday October 26, 1862

My dear Mother,
I received your ever welcome letter this morning & I take this opportunity of answering it as we are exempt from all duty today. I received two papers with the letter & was very glad to get them for it seems like home to read them. Oh how I would like to spend the winter at home but the prospect aint very encouraging now for that. Sometimes I think our Generals don't want to end this war as long as they can keep it up. You say the general opinion of the soldiers around there is the war wont last more than three months more. They have a different opinion of the war than I have. If they have to end this war by fighting it wont be ended for three years. But it is my candid opinion that three months more will bring a change. I have thought for some time that before three months they will complamize or acknowledge the Southern Confederacy & my belief is stronger now than ever for every one knows that after this war is over we will keep a strong standing army & there is recruiting officers around here now for the regular army. What is that for. There was an order read to us the other day that there would be recruiting officers here in a few days & all that wanted to join the regulars to give in their names the next day but they did not get many. If they get me in the regular it will be when I am drunk. I have got my foot in it as deep as I want it.
It is getting to be pretty cold weather here now. Last night we had quite a snow storm. I have bought an overcoat so I wont want that one at home. I thought it would be as cheap to buy one here. We are drawing winter clothes now.

I have not heard from Will since that one he mentioned in his letter. I expect he is on a march.

Austin Hudson expects to go home in a few days. The boys says that Sam was slightly wounded & sent north.

The pay rolls are made out & we expect to get paid off the first of next month. You mentioned in your last letter about so many coming home. I think sometimes that I don't want to go home till I can stay but I would like very well to see you all. I expect we will winter here for we are ditching our camp & making preparations for wet weather.

You need not send any more stamps till I write for some more for I have a plenty now. I don't write as much as I did for all the girls have quit writing to me.

Oh how I would like to see little Fred. I can imagine I see him beating his drum. I dreamed of seeing him the other night & only wish it was so.

Write in your next letter how they was getting along with the Mill when Pa left. Tell Mat & Lydia to write to me.

Well I dont know of anything to write of importance so I will close by stating that I am well & hope this will find you all the same.

My love to you all.

Your soldier boy

Geo Waterman

S Church

#59

Camp near Grand Junction, Tenn.
Nov 16th/62

Dear Mother,

I now seat myself to answer your letter of the 6th which I received in due time & was very glad to hear from you & to hear that you was having a good visit in the country.

I got a letter from Mat a few days before I got yours.

Just 16 months ago yesterday I went to Cutler Station & put my name down as a member of Co. K. To look back it don't seem but a little while & my time is most half out.

We expected to have a hard fight at Holly Springs but the report is that the rebels have left there & our men have possession of the place. We are camped about five miles south of Grand Junction & just about a half mile in Mississippi. We are in the rear of the whole army in this expedition. We have always been in the advance till this time but that was on account of being under the ranking General. General Rosecrans has left us & our division commander (General Stanley) has left us. We have been under him ever since the battle of New Madrid. We all hated to have him leave us. He thought a good deal of the Ohio brigade.

We heard that McClellan was removed from his command & Burnsides takes his place. I cant see the use of changing Generals so often. I dont believe it is good policy but then one half of the leading men are fighting for money. If they had to put up with the privates fare this war would have been ended long ago. They may talk of the Southern Soldiers geting sick of this war but if there aint as many in the Northern army sick of it I'll treat. If things dont work a little different we wont have any army before long. There was about 18 deserted out of this Regt while we was coming from Corinth down here: Two out of this Co.

We haven't been paid off yet & no sign of it at the present. What we are going to do down here is hard to tell but I think we will move on to Holly Springs & very likely we will stay there a while.

I have a coat here that I want to send home. If I was at home & had it there I would not take twelve dollars for it. It is an officers coat. It did not cost me much but I came honestly by it. I dont care if you send me a few more stamps for if we aint paid soon I cant get any here.

Well I don't know of any thing more to write so I will close by stating that I am well & hope this will find you all the same.

Your son Geo Waterman

S R C

Letter # 60

Camp near Grand Junction, Tenn
Nov 23rd 1862

Dear Mother,
I received your letter of the 16th in due time. I was very glad to hear from you & to hear that you was all well. I am enjoying good health at present & hope this will find you all the same. You stated in your letter that it had been two weeks since you had heard from me. That was while we was on that March. We left Corinth on Sunday the day that I always write to you & then it was a week before I had a chance to write. So that made two weeks that I did not write. We are moving around so much that I don't have much chance to write. So if you don't hear from me regular you must not feel uneasy. We are moving on toward Holly Springs as fast as we can fix the railroad. It is the opinion of the people here that we will not have no fight here but it is hard to tell what they will do. But I think we have the dead word on them here for there is or a large force moving down the Mississippi River to come in the rear of them & we have a pretty large army here. So I think the prospect is good for cleaning them out down here & go to Jackson, Miss. Some prophecies that the war is nearer to an end now than it ever was but I cant see no sign of an end yet. But I do hope it will soon end for I want to get into the United States once more where a fellow will be at liberty to breath without being guarded. If I was to be set free now I would not know what to do but I hope I will soon have the trial of it.
Tell Mis Simms that George is well & hearty. He says that he don't want me to write so often to you for his Mother wants him to write as often as I do to you. Geo used to call me his Pomeroy friend & I go by the name of Pomeroy now.
We are not paid off yet & I don't know when we will be. We are about all out of money now send me a few stamps in your letter next time you write. Write if you have heard from Will lately. He did not answer my last letter & I don't know where he is now.
Well I have no news to write & I want to answer Rhonda's letter. I will not write more at present.

Your son,

Geo Waterman
S.R.C.

Mississippi
Camp near Holly Springs
Dec ?ⁿᵈ/62

Dear Mother,
As I have a few idle hours I thought I would write you a few lines to let you
know that I am alive and well and hope this will find you all the same. It
has been some more than a week since I wrote but we have been marching
so much lately that I have not had time to write. We are now about five
miles south of Holly Springs and expect to move on in a few days. I
expected we would have a hard fight here but the rebels have left and I
expect we will have to run after them. I don't believe they will stand and
fight anymore. I would about as soon as fight them as to run them so much.
The talk is that we will move on to Jackson before long if it don't set in wet
weather. We made a reconnoisence the other day and drove the rebels into
their forts and the next day they left and it is supposed they went to
Grenada but if they won't fight us here they won't fight us there. Oh how I
wish this war was over and we could all go home. The prospects is fair now
but how long it will be so is hard to tell but one thing certain they are gone
up on the western and southern states & I am in hopes Burnsides will
crowd the thing in Va. One month from yesterday the Presidents
Proclamation takes affect. If they come back they will have to do it before
long but I don't look for that. I have seen several of their papers lately & I
see by them that they are getting discouraged.
We don't get mail very often now since we moved. As soon as the cars get to
running down here we will get our mail regular. You may not get this for
some time but if you don't hear from very often now you must not feel
uneasy. It has been most two weeks since I have heard from you.
Will is at Jackson yet. I saw the brigade that his regt was in & they said
the 18ᵗʰ was left at Jackson for guards. The whole western army is here now
and I think it is the intention to push right on south while it is good
weather. Well don't know of any thing more to write so I will stop. Tell the

girls to write for they have nothing else to do. Kiss little Freddy for me. My
love to you all.

Your son Geo. Waterman
S.R.C.

Dec 9th 1862
On picket Guard Near Waterford Miss.

Dear Mother.
I take my seat on the ground with a shingle for a writing desk to answer
your letter which I received in due time & was glad to hear that you were
all well. I am in excellent health at present & hope this will find you all
the same.
it is most beautiful weather here now. Most as warm as summer except at
night. we are having just the best of times here now. our guard duty is light
& we are camped in the woods & no drill ground handy so we don't have
much of it to do. there is a fair prospect of us staying here some time but it
is hard to tell what we will do. I think our hard times is about ended for
the rebels are pretty well discouraged in this part of the world.

Sometimes when I think of home I get most homesick & think it will be a
long time before we will get to go home but I think the prospect is very
encouraging at present more so than it has been for some time. the citizens
here say they wont fight us any more down here. the day you wrote your last
letter we were laying under the fire of the rebel guns but no one was hurt.
they had fortifications on both sides of the Tallahatchi river & then would
not stand a fight. You wanted to know if I knew of the 16th Ill. I have not
seen it since we were at Clear Creek. it aint in this division now. I received
them stamps & that pen. it is a good pen but most to course. I got two
papers with the last letter & was very glad to get them for it seems so much
like home to read them. I have sold that coat that I was going to send home.
it cost me about 2 dollars & I sold it for 9. I thought I had better sell it for
I had no chance to send it home. I am glad Pa has got in to steady work &
a fellow is doing well when he is making $1.25 a day these hard times.

We have not been paid off yet & I don't expect we will be for some time but we will get quite a pile when we do get it. I have a poor chance to write so you must excuse my poor writeing. as there is no news to write I will close. tell the girls I will write some in this letter if the mail don't go out too soon.

No more at present

Your Son Geo Waterman

S R C

Mother

You will see by the heading of my letter that we were camped near Waterford. Well we aint there now. We have moved a little higher down now about 25 miles. You see I wrote that there was a fair prospect of us stoping where we were for some time. Now see where we are. I had not wrote it more than 5 hours till we got marching orders & left there before I had a chance to send my letter out. we are now at Oxford a very beautiful country town. I will not pretend to say how long we will stay here for I wrote before & we left before I sent my letter out. that is the reason you don't hear from me regular so don't feel uneasy about me. we met about 750 prisoners while we were coming down here. they were taking them North. Excuse my other letter for I wrote it on a shingle. No more this time. Your loving Son Geo W / SRC

Oxford Miss

Dec 20/62

Dear Mother.

As I have plenty of time & nothing to busy myself with I thought I could not spend my time any better than by writing to you. It has been most two weeks since I have had a letter from home but I think it is no fault of yours. We don't get mail very regular now for there is no regular train here. When you will get this is more than I can tell for they are fighting at Jackson Tenn so the cars wont be running past here for a few days. this brigade has gone up there to reinforce them. you will perhaps wonder why I aint with them this time. we was wakened up about ten oclock in the night with orders to be ready to march by 12 with three days rations & 70 rounds of cartridges. the boys thought they was going on a force March & did not want to take all their clothes so they left some of their blankets & things & left one man in each mess to take care of them & as I had the sick head ache the Orderly Sargeant told me to stay. I don't like to stay behind every time there is a prospect for a fight for the boys will think I am a coward. I don't like to fight any better than any body els but I would rather do it than be called a coward. to tell the truth I am tired of this kind of work & am anxious for the war to end. I am not home sick but sick of the war & I am not the only one in that fix either but we are in it now & the only thing we can do is to stay in it till we can get out. I think if the leading men in both armies were as anxious for peace as the soldiers are this war would end soon. and another thing if they were not making more than the soldiers are it would not have lasted this long and doubtful whether there would have been any war. I believe it was got up for a speculation & nothing els. to a young man that has no trade or no start in business this three years is that much of his life lost. the very prospect is pretty good in Va now. I am in hopes he will do something for the whole thing depends on his movement. we heard they had taken Fredericksburg & burned it & that Burnsides had possession of their earth works but how true it is we don't know.

You mentioned in one of your letters about them socks that Mrs Lawrence was knitting for Arthur whether they come through & what they cost. they come through but I don't know what they cost for there was no stamps on them. you said you would send me some if I wanted them. I don't think I will need them for we have a chance to draw them whenever we want to. Our Capt has been at home & he brought 25 pair of boots & will take some of the socks if I can get them.

We have not been paid off yet & I don't think we will now till the first of next year then there will be six months pay due us. I shall try & send about $50 home. I will have to keep some in case of necessity & buy my bacca with.

I have seen as much of the South as I want to see. I would not give them old rocks back of Pomeroy for the whole Southern Confederacy & be compeled to live here if it is all like what I have seen. the country is generally hilly & sandy. Not much difference in the country here & in

Ohio but a good deal of difference in the climate & the inhabitance. the climate is a good deal warmer than it is in Ohio but as for the people here (what few there is left) they are of a colder nature especially towards us. the country aint very thickly settled but when you do come to a plantation you will generaly see a very nice house with about 25 or 30 negro huts around it. expect to see Uncle Tom's Cabin yet before I go home. Holly Springs is about as nice a town as I ever saw. All nice houses & the yards filled with as nice shrubbery as I ever saw but I tell you the population was small at the time we went through there. the most of the citizens were in Oxford when we come in but they did not seem to be pleased with our visit. You will perhaps think paper is not very plenty down here by this & you will think about right for this is all the paper I have at present but it is as good to write on as any paper. we have just heard that they were fighting at Corinth. the 2d brigade has just struck tents & are preparing to leave. I would not wonder if they were having hot times at Corinth & Jackson. Well I dont know of anything more to write that will be interesting to you. so I will close by stating that I am well & hope this will find you all the same. no more at present but remain

your loving Son
Geo Waterman
S R C

8

INTRODUCTION TO THE 1863 LETTERS

"Wm Rainier was killed at the battle of Murfreesboro. His brother Curtis is in this Co he feels the worst kind about his brother."
– George W. Waterman, February 5, 1863 (Corinth, Mississippi)

For Private George Waterman, 1863 began guarding company property at Oxford, Mississippi, where the 39th Ohio had stopped during a foraging expedition in search of food and other necessities for the army. The regiment's intended quest had been interrupted by reports from General Grant's headquarters that Confederate General Bedford Forrest with an estimated command of five to seven thousand men had crossed the Tennessee River on December 15. On the 18th, George's Company K with the 39th had received orders to march with three days rations and seventy cartridges for every man, as Grant intended to drive Forrest back across the river. George had been selected by his officers to stay behind as the rest marched off in search of the enemy. On December 31 at Parker's Cross Roads the command including Fuller's Ohio Brigade surprised and defeated the Confederates, who quickly retreated, leaving many prisoners in Union hands. George, once again having missed an opportunity to engage the enemy, worried others would label him a coward, which he disdained more than going into battle.

The enemy routed, the army was ordered back to Corinth where they arrived on January 9. The march was strenuous as the roads were covered with ice and mud. Cold weather including intermittent rain and snow had enveloped the countryside, reminding the soldiers of the march to St. Louis the previous spring. Many officers said the two hundred miles covered within two weeks' time was the hardest march of any army during the war. Upon the Brigade's arrival on the 9th, although the garrison was on half rations, General Dodge ordered they receive full rations as the men were so depleted from the last twenty days of severe service. Despite the terrible march, most men were in high spirits having given Forrest and his boys a thrashing. Fortunately George also missed this terrible ordeal as once again his detail to stay at Oxford had saved him. He, with others detached, returned to Corinth a day later on January 10.

For the remainder of January through early April, the men busied themselves acquiring material to enhance their camp at Corinth. On April 13 the Brigade, this time with George along, commenced a twenty-day raid into Alabama through the Cherokee and Choctaw Valleys, afterwards returning to Corinth before moving to Memphis, Tennessee, in May. The regiment stayed on duty at Memphis through October when they were sent to Prospect, Tennessee, but yet again without George who had by doctor's orders been sent to hospital #2 at Paducah, Kentucky. In late December he was sent further north and nearer home with a transfer to Camp Dennison, ironically where he was mustered into Company K in 1861.

Private Waterman spent most of 1863 idle in camp or later convalescing in hospitals. Both allowed lots of time to write home. His lengthy letters from this period give insight on his thoughts and how they had changed since the early days in Missouri. At times he was clearly discouraged that no end to the conflict was in sight, and also relayed his disgust at the changing cast of generals, whom he feared had more interest in furthering careers than in executing and ending the war. He was especially derisive of the eastern campaign: "they fight in the east for the name & money not for their country."

Reports containing excessive casualties like those from General Ambrose Burnside's fiasco at the Battle of Fredericksburg, Virginia, where the Union Army suffered over 12,500 casualties, shocked and disheartened the men. Nearer in Tennessee, casualty numbers from the battle of Stone's River at Murfreesboro exceeded 25,000 soldiers for both armies, which further demoralized the troops. Little did anyone know then that the casualty list of 1863 would dwarf those earlier numbers. At Gettysburg over 50,000 men were killed, captured, missing, or wounded. Combined casualties at the battles of Chancellorsville, Virginia, and Chickamauga, Georgia neared 60,000.

Alonzo Simms of the 33rd OVI. Married George's sister Lydia Waterman. Wounded at Chickamauga.

It was at the September 19 and 20 battle of Chickamauga that Sergeant Alonzo F. Simms, while serving with the 33rd Ohio Infantry, was wounded when a Rebel conical shaped bullet entered just in front of his left ear traversing out under the nose through the center of his upper lip. At the time of his wounding he was just another soldier from back home. But if George Waterman would have lived, Alonzo would have been his brother-in-law. Alonzo married George's sister Lydia in 1870 at Pomeroy, Ohio. Miraculously, Alonzo returned to his regiment by the end of 1863 and was promoted a 1st Lieutenant at war's end.

George's sister Lydia Waterman Simms

Eva Simms, daughter of Alonzo and Lydia Simms

Chain of artifacts collected by Alonzo
Simms on Sherman's March to the Sea

Letter from Eva Simms to Flora
Hetzer, explaining how she came to
give Frank Schwartz her father's
collected artifacts from Sherman's
March to the Sea

Juxtaposed with these fierce and bloody battles was one bit of good news: January 1, 1863, marked the end of slavery in the South when President Lincoln's Emancipation Proclamation took effect. The Proclamation was preliminarily issued in September as a warning to the South to end the rebellion no later than the close of 1862 or President Lincoln would free three and a half million slaves within the boundaries of those states in rebellion. The Confederacy of course refused, and in an extraordinary use of his war powers, Lincoln thus declared that all southern slaves "shall be then, thenceforward, and forever free," striking a blow to the Confederacy with his emergency measure and bringing the abolition of slavery to the forefront of the war effort. In his book *Lincoln's Emancipation Proclamation*, Allen Guelzo points out that "without the Proclamation, the Confederacy even in defeat would have retained legal title to its slaves..." In addition, Union troops were now permitted to accept freed and runaway slaves into their army. (Slavery was officially abolished nationally in December 1865, with the ratification of the 13th Amendment to the U.S. Constitution.)

As Union regiments moved deeper into the South during 1863, they bore witness to the prevalence of poverty and starvation in the Rebel cities and countryside. George observed that many southerners lived on corn bread made without salt and used scorched meal as a substitute for coffee. "If you find any person that wants to buy the Southern Confederacy," he writes, "tell them to bring down a bag of salt and a little coffee and I will insure them to get it."

George Waterman rarely discussed politics in his letters home, but was very clear in his opinion of the "Copperhead" anti-war Democrat congressman from his home state of Ohio, Clement Vallandigham. Court martialed for opposing the war and exiled to the Confederacy in 1863, Vallandigham, who was running for governor of Ohio in absentia from Canada, was considered by George to be a traitor to his country, along with anyone who would support him. To make his point, George stated he would vote for Jeff Davis before he would ever cast one for Vallandingham.

Also in his 1863 correspondence, George relayed his thoughts on the war in general and of course mentioned most major battles. The surrender of the city of Vicksburg, Mississippi, to General Grant on

Pomeroy, Ohio historical marker, Morgan's Raid, 1863

July 4 coincided with Lee's Army of Northern Virginia retreating from Pennsylvania after Gettysburg. Surprisingly, in his July 6 letter home, George wrote, "reports says that Lee and Meade have had a fight and that Lee got defeated," yet he was not aware that Vicksburg had already fallen. Most news picked up by the soldiers was through newspapers distributed in every town and camp. It was through papers the men of southern Ohio counties learned of Confederate General John Hunt Morgan's Ohio raid that month as well.

"The Morgan raid is the topic of conversation here at present. he has just been in the part of the county where our Co was got up," wrote George on July 28. In this letter he clearly relays concern for his family and home in Pomeroy, knowing the Confederate cavalry had recently passed through.

By the end of 1863, George wrote more freely about his health and less about the war. A sense of hope returned to his writings as the Christmas holidays approached, most probably bolstered by the few gifts that came his way, or perhaps knowing he was back in Ohio was all he needed. By late December, he was hoping to be discharged or transferred to the Invalid Corps.

9

THE 1863 LETTERS

22

Corinth, Miss. Jan 11, 1863

Dear Mother.
You will perhaps think it very strange that you have not heard from me for
some time but believe me it is not my fault. I wrote a letter while we were at
Grand Junction but I don't know whether you got it or not if you did you
will know the fix we have been in.
We left the Junction a few days after I wrote & got to Corinth the 13th &
before I had time to write we got orders to go foraging. We got back last
night & this is the first time I have had a chance to write. We have orders
to be ready to move at any time now. it is supposed we are going to
Memphis, a part of the 2d brigade started this morning. we will not be apt
to go for a few days.
we are having the most disagreeable weather we have had this winter. it has
rained & snowed for the last week & we are camped on a level piece of
ground so you can imagine what kind of a camp we have, it is raining
today & it is very disagreeable in the tents, but such is a soldiers life. O
when will this war end, it seems to me that it never will. We was all
rejoicing over the news that we heard from Vicksburg but when we heard
that it was not taken & that Sherman had fallen back to Memphis we
changed our tunes. I never seen the boys so mad and discouraged, if my
patriotism was all in one lump now it would not be as large as a pea. I am
well convinced that our Generals are not trying to end this war. they spend
all the time in changing Generals. I tell you the men wont stand it much
longer, if this army had been called out for 12 or 18 months the war would

*have been over by this time for they would have tried & done something.
I got a letter from you last night which makes four that I have got since I
wrote. You wanted me to write how I fared. We have plenty to eat such as
crackers coffee tea sugar rice meat of all kinds beans & plenty of clothes
but rather short of money. there is little prospect of being paid off now. we
have signed the pay rolls several days ago but when we will get our money is
more than I can tell. we only get two months pay this time but there is six
months pay due us. why they don't pay us up is more than I can tell. I
would not wonder if this would be the last time we will be paid off while
we are in the army.*

*our Regt went through Jackson the other day but I was not with it. Arthur
saw Will, said he was well & fat as a hog. if we go to Memphis we will be
apt to go by there. I don't see why he don't write oftner. I got a letter from
Jas. Davis the other day. he is near Charleston, Va. there is a fellow in the
27th Ohio that lives where Uncle Reuben taught school. he said the last he
heard of him he was at Cattlesburg Ky. this fellows name is Worthington.
he has just lately come out. well I will have to stop writing for it is raining
& the tent leaks on my paper so I can hardly write. tell the girls that I will
write to them some other time. they must not think hard of me for not
writing this time. I will close by stating that I am in good health & hope
this will find you all the same. I was sorry to hear that you was not very
well. dont work more than you can without hurting you for you have plenty
of help. No more this time but remain your loving Son.*

Geo Waterman
SC

#66

Corinth, Mississippi
Feb 5/63

*Dear Mother
I received a letter from you a few days ago & would have answered it
sooner but I have had a bad cold for a few days and my head has not felt
much like writing but as I have plenty of time today I thought I would try
and write. I was glad to hear that you had got my letter for I know you*

would feel uneasy about me till you did hear from me. I wrote a letter while we were at Oxford & did not get to send it till I got to the junction but I don't think you got that one. you said you was afraid that Will was in that battle at Murfreesboro but I don't think he was for our Regt was through there a few days before the fight & Arthur saw Will. a part of the 18th is mounted & they have them for scouting & the rest of them are Provost guards at Jackson. I wrote a letter to Will a few days ago but it aint time for an answer yet.

Wm Rainier was killed at the battle of Murfreesboro. his brother Curtis is in this Co he feels the worst kind about his brother.

Corinth Mississippi
Feb 9 '63 *

Dear Mother,

Your letter of the 25th came safe to hand last night & I take this earliest opportunity of answering it. I am enjoying good health at present and hope this may find you all the same.

We are still in our old nest but expecting to leave soon but may not go for some time. Yesterday we got orders to be ready to move out at a minutes notice but the order now countermanded in about two hours but we don't know how soon we will get another.

When we are in camp I will write regular but when we are on the march it is impossible to write.

You spoke about not getting mail regular from me. It is account the R.R. they have not finished it through the Columbus Ky yet sometimes we don't get any mail here for a week but most of the time we get mail regular. I hope the time will soon come when we can converse face to face and not be obliged to compare our thoughts in the small space of a sheet of paper but I am very glad we have that privilege.

I saw Mr. Simms and Jacob both when they was over to our camp. We were camped within ¾ of a mile to them for some time. I was glad to hear that you had heard from Will. I wrote a letter to him the other day and told him he ought to write oftener than he did. I would like to have seen him when our regt went through Jackson but I saved a hard march by not going. That was the hardest march our Regt has ever been on but they saved the day by getting there as they did. A good many of them did come back barefoot but they come through on the cars as soon as they got to the R.R. A part of the time they had nothing but a pint of meal a day & done some tall marching on that. I tell you I am proud of the Ohio brigade. They have done as much hard marching as any other brigade and are always willing & ready to do their duty. Some of them I am sorry to say lost all their patriotism while they was on that hard march & took a notion to leave. 40 of our Regt deserted that time. Our Col has gone home and he says he will bring them back if he finds them.

You said that you heard that the 21st Va. Regt had started for Corinth. They have not come here but I heard they had gone to Memphis. I would like to see the boys in them regts very well but I don't think they will come here. My (?) that I spoke about is well now. It did not last very long & I was glad when it was gone.

What is the general opinion there about arming the negroes. Some of the soldiers don't like it & think it is all right. The war has come to such a pitch that it is immaterial to me how they end it. I never thought it would turn out as it has when I left home. However right or wrong they are arming & drilling the negroes here. I hope it may turn out all right and peace be speedily restored to our distracted country.

No more at present but remain your loving Son Geo. W. Waterman
S.R.C.

P.S. I did not get them two papers you sent with the letter but expect I will get them the next mail. G.W.

* Pension Letter #2

Corinth Mississippi
Feb 18th/63

Dear Mother
I received your letter of the 2d this morning & I now hasten to answer it. I am enjoying excellent health now & hope this may find you all the same.

I was sorry to hear that you do not get letters from me regular. I think the RR will soon be repaired so the mail will go through regular. I have wrote every week since we have been in this camp but they are a long time going through.

we have been in this camp longer than I expected we would when we came here & I hope we will remain here some time for we are fixed comfortable now & it would be hard marching now for we have had a good deal of rain lately. I did think for some time that we would be ordered to Vicksburg but I don't think we will go now at least I hope not for I expect they will have a hard fight there. they have taken a good many troops away from here so I think what is here now will be apt to stay here some time.

you spoke about our men going to take the capital of Miss. if we get Vicksburg Jackson is as good as ours for they cant hold Jackson when Vicksburg is in our possession. we were moving on to Jackson but did not get farther than Oxford when the rebbels got in our rear & we had to fall back. if it had not been for that I expect we would have been to Jackson by this time.

O how I wish this war was ended. I am geting tired of it & very anxious for it to end but God only knows when it will. sometimes I think there will be a proposition of peace made when the new congress sets which is the 4th of next month. if it is settled it is very doubtfull whether it is settled satisfactory or not.

I hope we will be taken no farther south this summer for it is hot enough where we are to do me but we will stand it better this summer than we did last for we have got used to it. we have had no cold weather here this winter to speak of & it has the apearance of spring here now.

about all we have to do now is to haul lumber. our Regt was out the other day & we had rather a hard time of it. we was gone most four days & it rained most all the time. the people in the north may think they see hard times but if they should see some of the families in this state. all they have to live on is corn bread & no salt to put in it & all the coffee they have is scorched meal. we were rather short of grub when we were gone so we bought a chicken & three corn cakes & they charged a dollar for them. they are the most ignorant set of people I ever saw. One man asked us how it come that they whiped us all the time. they can be made to believe anything. one thing I noticed they was very anxious to get hold of our money. I thought they had not much confidence in their money. we couldn't make them believe this postage currency was good for anything.

Thursday, 19th

as I have a little time now I will finish my letter. we are cutting timber now preparatory to building us a log cabin. our tent leaks so bad that we concluded to put us up a house. it will be a joke on us if we have to leave when we get it built. by ½ days work I have found that work gives a fellow an appetite. if we had a little work to do every day we would feel better & be healthier than we are laying around in camp. the health of the troops is good at present.

I have not had a letter from Will yet. it is time I had an answer from my letter that I wrote to him. I don't see why he don't write more than he does. I don't know when I can send this for I have no stamps but will borrow one if I can. it is impossible to get stamps here now. well we will soon have battallion drill so I will close. hoping to hear from you soon again I will close by signing myself your loving son. Geo Waterman

SRC

N B if you find any person that wants to buy the Southern Confederacy tell them to bring down a bag of salt & a little coffee & I will insure them to get it.

#67

Corinth, Mississippi
March 3d/63

My Dear Mother,

Your letter of the 22d was received last night & I now take this opportunity of answering it. I am enjoying good health at present & hope this will find you all the same.

this day will ever be remembered by me. one year ago today we marched to New Madrid. there it was we had the first shot fired at us. we marched up within ¼ of a mile of the river & it at that time was bank full so the guards of a steamboat was level with the bank. imagine the Ohio river bank full & a gunboat anchored close to shore & a brigade moving in line of battle across the bottom over in Mason City & you can form some kind of an idea of the fix, we were in one year ago today. there was a corn field between us & the river & we thought it was fun to see the shells making the corn stalks fly. we was not sensible of the danger we were in it being the first time we were under fire. we were there 10 days only till we had possession of the place. on the 19th we marched into the Fort. that was the beginning of our hard times. you said that I had said nothing about being paid off. we were paid off over two months ago. I thought I had mentioned it. I sent $10 & a receipt of Thos. Hudsons. Arthur & I owed Tom somewhere near $25 & we paid him $20 when he was at our camp last May. I sent the receipt & $10 & told you to settle with some of the Hudsons folks but I am afraid you will not get it. if the receipt is lost we will not have anything to show that we have paid him unless they will take our word for it. we are expecting to be paid off again soon for we have been mustered & have signed the pay rolls. there is six months pay due us but they say we aint going to be paid for only two months. I shall send all I can home. I think I will get a check this time. everything is so dear down here that if a fellow buys much he will have to have plenty of money. I bought a pair of boots & had to give $7.50 for them. about 20 of us sent north for some boots & we were to give $5.00 a pair for them & run our own risk of getting them & while our Capt was at home he started them to us but we never got them.

What do people think about this conscription act that has passed. I think it is a very good thing but it will go hard with a good many that cant raise $300. there is some that I know of that I would like to see packing a knapsack. one fault I have with it is it gives the rich a chance & the poor none.

I am glad that Pa has no notion of moving out west. I wish he could sell his share of the mill & get it paid for.

I got them stamps that you sent but I never got the two last papers you sent. you need not send any more papers for a fellow in the same mess that I am in has sent for it for six months. I am sorry that Branch will not sell any stamps to send off. it is hard to get stamps here & I don't think there is any way to send letters without stamps.

in my last letter to you I told you we were going to put us up a house. we have got it up & we live in style. we are fixed comfortable now. our Col has been home & got back night before last. it is the report now that they are going to give furloughs. going to let 7 men go out of every 100. how true it is I don't know. two men out of our Co. are at home now. they live on Shade river close to Chester. their name is Comstock. they are Brothers.

I got a letter from Mattie but I have not time to answer it now. tell the girls they must not think hard of me if I don't answer every letter, they have a better chance to write than I have & then there is three to one which aint fair you know. but I shall write as often as I can to all of you. tell Lydia that I would be pleased to hear from her. she never wrote but one & I answered that.

Well it will soon be drill time so I will bring my letter to an end. My love to you all.

    Your loving son, Geo Waterman

        Corinth, Mississippi
        March 9th 1863 *

My Dear Mother,

I received a letter from you last night after we had all gone to bed but I was very glad to get up to read a letter from home.

I am well as common & hope this will find you all the same. I hardly know what to write for there has nothing new transpired here for a long worthy of notice, if you take the commercial you will see how we spent Washingtons birthday and also some speeches made by some officers of this brigade. You mentioned in your letter that you sent me your last commercial. I did not get it but we get papers here every day so you need not send me any more papers. It is the daily or the weekly com that you take. The daily is the best-there is persons in this brigade that are correspondents for the daily com so if you take that you will hear often from this brigade which I know will be interesting to you.

We were paid off again the 7th of this month. I have $25.00 to send home the first good opportunity I have to send it; we expect to be paid off again in a short time so I will wait a while & if there is any prospect of being paid soon I will wait and send it all together.

I shall not trust any more in letters for there is so many scoundrels watching for such a chance that it is not safe anymore. I know of several in this regt that had money sent to them and they never got it.

I am glad Aunt Henrietta got my picture. I should have sent it to everyone I know of now. I am sorry to hear that the small pox is around there now. Be very careful that none of you gets it. there was a fellow in our co had it- while we were at New Madrid but they took him off before he gave it to any person.

We are enjoying ourselves the best kind here now. We are fixed up comfortable now for the first time since we were at Clear Creek & time passes off fast-with & easy with us now. We are all confident of staying here for some time. we have been on the go every since we left-clear creek till we came here and it is to be hoped now that we will have a little rest.

We got into a little argument last night about Racine. I with some of the rest sayed that Racine used to go by some other name & we went through it was Graham Station. I told them that Pa would know for he had lived there for 25 years now we want to know if the name was changed & what it went by at first – if it has been changed.

The main talk is now all about furloughs. Our Col says as soon as it becomes a law he will begin to give furloughs. The question now is whether it will become a law or not. I should be very happy to take a trip home, but our time is fast running out. We have got to the top of the hill have commenced to go down the other side. Our time commenced at the 8th of July/61, that was when the regiment was organized.

If them copperheads in the north only knew how patriotic they was making the soldiers they would not be enterprising in their wicked purposes. If the soldiers would only get at them once they would soon clean them out. Some of the I'lls men here offer their services free if they will let them go back and clean out the state. I am very much in favor of this conscription act. I like to see them shell out.

Well as I said before I have no news to write so I will bring my letter to a close. Write soon to your loving son Geo Waterman S.R.C Pomeroy

*Pension Letter #3

#70

Corinth, Mississippi
March 19ᵗʰ/63

My Dear Mother,
I received your letter of the 8ᵗʰ night before last & I intended to answer it
yesterday while on picket but it was to hot & I had no good place to write.
I wrote to Lydia yesterday while on guard. We have just come off of guard
& got our breakfast & I thought I would answer your letter so it would go
out today for it has been some over a week since I have wrote.
I am still enjoying good health & hope this may find you all in like
circumstances. we are having the best kind of times here now. we enjoy our
selves as well as we did at Palmyra & we have about as good quarters. our
Regt have got all their houses up & the 27ᵗʰ & 63d are building now. we
will have quite a town here before long. O, how I would like to have you
visit us & see how we live. it would be quite a sight for one that never saw
a huge camp. the troops here are in tolerable good & fine spirits. The
Knights of the G.C. and the Northern Sympathizers are entirely mistaken
in their work for instead of sowing disloyalty among the troops they are
making them more patriotic if they knew how many curses & threats are
heaped on them they would tremble in their boots at the sight of a soldier.
they will see the time that they will not dare to talk as they do now. they
will have soldiers to deal with & citizens.
Mother I am discouraged disappointed & angry; you will perhaps wonder
what at, I will tell you; I am angry on account of being duned for money &
disappointed in sending money home & discouraged because I cant make
more. you must not think I am extravagant with my money (I don't say
that you do) for to sum it all up I have not spent much; when I bought the
half of that mill L. Mitchell had paid some 25 or $30 toward it besides
his work & I think he charged $50 for his claim on it; we paid him about
up before we left. when we were at Palmyra he wrote me a letter & said
there was a little coming to him yet & requested me to send him some when
we were paid off; I did not know how much we owed him so I sent him $30
& thought sure it would be enough. a few nights ago I received a letter from
him stating that there was $25 coming to him & he would like to have it.
I have got 25 or 30 dollars that I intended to send home the first good

chance I had, now I am disappointed; thank God he has nothing to show that I have bought him out & if he does any thing unfair about it he wont benefit any by my labor. say nothing about it to anybody. I shall send as much home as I can & try to have enough to run away on when I get home, ha, ha. Well my paper is most full so I will close. Your son Geo W.

S R C

our Cols. name is Edwin F. Noyes.

Corinth, Mississippi
March 25th/63

Dear Mother,
I received your letter of the 15th on the night of the 23d. I was sorry to hear of your poor health but hope you will not be sick. I am in tolerable good health & hope this may find you all the same.
Curtis Comstock has got back to the Co he brought a letter for me from Lewis & Jane. they say they have had a great meeting going on at Bethel. Lewis is not very punctual in writing to me. I got a letter from him while at Clear Creek then I did not get another till we came here this last time & still they find fault because I don't write oftener.
I am glad that Mr. Comstock speaks so highly of me. it is more than I can say of him & say the truth. there is not many in the Co that likes him. I hope you may never hear any other kind of a report from me than what you have heard. I try to conduct myself where ever I am the same that I would if I was at home. I have been favored some in this Co but still I have done a good deal of marching. He is mistaken when he says I am the smallest man in the Co. there is several smaller than I am. I believe if I should try I could keep off of most every march but I will not shirk from duty when I am able to do & keep my end up.
I expect the spring campaign will soon commence if it keeps good weather, whether we will take an active part in it or not I don't know. Sometimes I think we will remain here the most of the summer then again it looks sometimes as if we would soon be ordered off but there is no more troops here now than ought to be all the time. an expedition of mounted infantry is sent out from here every little while. three Regts left the other day

mounted on mules, whether we will be called on to go or not I don't know. we seem to be kind of an independent Brigade at present. dont belong to any division in particular. our old division all went to Vicksburg but this brigade. & that march to the Tenn river was all that kept us from going. we came back here all ragged & worn out about the time so many troops was ordered away from here. we were in no condition for marching so soon. I think there is going to be some fighting done in Ky before long. some think we will be ordered there but I hardly think we will. I think old Rosecrans will give them all they want. he is one of the fighting men. O how I would like to see such fellows as Hod Atkins in the army & on a force March. it would do me good. I see by the papers that the citizens are going to try to resist the arrest of deserters in Monroe Co., Ohio. they will have a good time of it I assure you. the military authorities aint to be fooled with much longer & the northern sympathizers will soon find it out. I see they don't have as much to say as they did for some time past. they aint having their desired affect on the army. the soldiers are a great deal more patriotic & determined than they was sometime ago.

I see by the papers that they are going to pay the troops up to the first of March which will be four months pay. we are having most beautiful weather here now. the trees are beginning to look quite green. I received a letter from Aunt Lo & Uncle Moses the other day. he wrote me a very serious letter. he has joined the church. I got them stamps you sent me, them you sent me & what I have got will last me sometime.

Well I have nothing more to write of importance so I will bring my letter to a close by signing myself your loving son.

Geo Waterman
S C

Corinth, Mississippi
March 30th/63

My Dear Mother
Your letter of the 22d came safe to hand last evening & I take this opportunity of answering it. I am enjoying tolerable good health with the exception of a cold that I have had for a few days past but is better now.

the weather is so changeable here at present that most of us have colds.
You wrote me a very encouraging letter & I am truly happy to receive such.
I am shure we have good reason to be encouraged at present. things begin to
look dark at present to the rebbels & they are so sensible of the fact that
they are beginning to own it. it is a fact too plain to be denied that
starvation is actualy stareing them in the face. they can face the cannon but
starvation will bring them to the scribe. I see in most every paper extracts
taken from Richmond papers that starvation is about to drive them from
their strong hold which the enemy has tried several times but failed.
Richmond will be evacuated in less than a month then look out in the
southwest, Ky & Tenn will be the principal battle fields here after. No
doubt but there will be another fight at this place before the war is over. If I
have to fight any more I want to do it here. Once inside of these
fortifications & I would feel safe. if they evacuate Vicksburg we may look
out for something to do here & if they evacuate Richmond there will be hot
work in Tenn & Ky. It looks to me as if we would stay here now for there
is no more troops here now than is necessary to hold the place. I don't care
if we stay the rest of our time here for we have a beautiful and good camp
here. the woods are quite green now & the peach trees have blossomed long
ago. Spring is considerable earlier here than it is in the north. I am
surprised to think that H. Smith has turned out to be a secesh. about as
good a Union speech as I ever heard made he made it on Tuppers Plains at
a pole raising.
We will soon be paid off again. they are making out the pay rolls now for
four months. I don't know how much I will be able to send home for I will
have to send some to L. Mitchell. Arthur got a letter from his Father the
other day. he writes very encouraging now about that Mill matter. he says
he has sold all the pine lumber & has been offered $10 per thousand for
the oak. he says that will more than pay what we owe Humphrey. We have
never got anything for what we sawed for Applegate & they all think he is
going to act the rascal with us. I think the old Hypocrite had a hand in
that affair with that fellow that run off with a part of our lumber. I
suppose you are aware that we give up the mill for what we owed on it so
that is paid for. Now we owe $300 to Humphrey & the same to Clark
besides some little dribs we have about 40 thousand feet of lumber beams,
at $70 per thousand and it will bring $200 & Applegate owes us between

*two & three hundred dollars & Woods about the same & I don't know
how much lumber we have left on forked run not knowing how much that
fellow run away with but we ought to have enough to bring $150 or 200
dollars. if every thing goes off right we will come out all strait & have a
little to spree on. if we have enough to clear us I will be satisfied to lose my
time.*

*I wrote you sometime ago about furloughs but I think there is nothing of it.
although the Col says he is looking every day for the order to give them. I
have not calculated on geting one so I will not be disappointed if I do not
get one. I would like the best kind to see all of you but when my time was
up to go back O how I would hate to leave. I have often thought of the
abrupt manner in which I left home. I did not realize the length of time I
might be gone. I hated to go as bad as you hated to have me but like
yourself I tried to hide my feelings as much as possible but after I was gone
I thought more seriously of the matter. I am glad, now that I came when I
did the way things has turned out. I shall try to serve my time out a true &
faithful soldier to be comforted by the thought that the time will come (if we
live) when we can all return home in peace & not be compelled to leave
home again under such circumstances. God grant that the time may soon
come. Well my fingers is most numb with cold so I will close by signing
myself your ever loving son.   Geo Waterman S Church*
*P.S. I was surprised to hear that Fred had learned to read. O, how I would
like to see the little fellow.*

#73

*Corinth, Mississippi
Apr 7th/63*

*My Dear Mother,
I have put off writing a few days over my regular time expecting to get a
letter from home but it has not come yet so I thought I would not wait any
longer. I shall look for a letter tonight.*
*We have had great times to-day. We raised a flag & had a great
celebration in honor of the battle of Shiloh one year ago yesterday & today
one of the bloodiest battles of this war was fought.*

All the troops about Corinth was brought as close to the pole as they could be got. the flag was run up & we gave three cheers then the band commenced to play the Star Spangled Banner & every battery about town fired the National salute which is 34 guns. the next was prayer & then a speech from Col Bane of the 50th Ills. he had his right arm shot off at the battle of Shiloh. that is the reason they appointed him to speak. he made an excellent speech & a very patriotic one but it was all Ills. with him. he spoke very encouraging about the war. he says that we are more capable of carrying on the war now than we were while the rebbels are geting weaker all the time. he went on to tell how our army & navy had increased since the war commenced & the improvements on arms & the great inventions that the Yankee has made in gun boats. he says the yankees has iron clads now that not only defyes the South but England & France & Johny Bull has give up beat & Prince Napoleon has run into his hole like a pararie gofer. he spoke a great deal about the copperheads & wanted to know what we thought of them. he said he would tell us what he thought of them & better to explain him-self he would relate an anecdote. He said there used to be a class of people believed in trans-substansiation that is they believed that when one person died there was another born & the soul of the dead person went to the new-born. Now, says he I think when these copperheads was born no body died.

Upon the whole we had a good time today. there has nothing of importance passed for the last week but reviewing the army. we have had two reviews this week. One today & I suppose it was as grand a military display as ever went off at this place. it was a grand sight & I just thought I would like to have you see it. everything has its charms, war with the rest. there is several in this Co. that gets some very insulting letters from some of the copperheads in the North. You know there was some talk of sending some soldiers north to enforce the conscription. Well there was a fellow in the Co got a letter from one of his butternut friends in the North & he told us to come on with our army if we wanted fun & that they had 250 thousand men ready to resist the draft. quite a threat but 25 men could run all they could raise. the mail has just come in but not distributed yet. I will soon know whether I will have a letter.

the mail has come in but no letter. I think I have missed one. I with 11 others are on a detail to build our Col. a house. we commence in the morning, it is now roll call & I wont have no time to write tomorrow so I will bring my letter to a close by hoping this will find you all as well as myself.

No more at present but remain your loving son

Geo Waterman

S R C

come to read this over I find I have not wrote much news.

#74

Corinth, Mississippi
Apr 12th/63

My Dear Mother

Your letter of the 19th is at hand. it was 12 days coming through. it has not been long since I wrote to you but I did not write much & as I have a good chance to write I thought I would answer your letter. I am in good health & sincerely hope this may find you the same but I am afraid you are not by the way you write. I am afraid you are sick & don't want me to know it but I hope not. You said you had been taking medicine some time & was geting better now. I hope you will soon get well again. dont work any while there is so many there to do the work.

A fellow in this Co takes the Telegraph & I see by it that they have had a little fight at the Pt Pleasant & the rebbels got repulsed. the people in Mason City had quite a scare. I don't like to hear that for it is getting most home.

I would not be surprised if we left here before long but we may not. the spring campaign will soon open now & we will very likely take a part in it. There has been some talk of us going to Florence, Ala but I don't know whether we will go or not. I think I would as soon be there as here in the summer it is beginning to be hot days here now so much so that the boys like to get on picket so as to be in woods which is green and comfortable now. such nice weather almost makes me home sick but we are doing very well at present. I don't see that there is much going on at present towards ending the war. it was rumored that our men had made an attack on Charleston but it was from rebel sources so it is not generally believed.

I am helping to build the Col. a house now to-day being Sunday we lay by. I have tried to draw off our camp so you can tell how we are situated. we are camped about 1 ½ miles south of Corinth the 27th on our right & the 63d on our left. we are just inside of the breastworks in front of the Regt. is what we call the Regimental parade ground. there is where we form the Regt for dress-parade. the space between to Companies is the Co parade ground. the Co is formed twice a day for roll call at 8 oclock in the evening & six in the morning. the house that I stay in is the first one on the color line & the first house built in the Regt.

We are expecting to be paid off soon. we signed the pay rolls most two weeks ago. I don't know why we have not been paid before this. I shall try to send some home when we are paid off.

Well I guess between the three letters I have wrote all I can think of so I will close. tell Freddy to hurry & learn to write so he can write me a letter. no more at present but remain your loving Son. Geo Waterman

S R C

Corinth, Mississippi
May 2nd / 63

My Dear Mother,
Once again I seat myself to pen a few lines to let you know that I am still alive & well & sincerely hope this may find you all the same. you will no doubt begin to feel a little uneasy by not hearing from me most two weeks. I believe I wrote my last letter that I thought we would soon get marching orders. I was right for on the 19th we got orders to be ready to march the next day with three days rations. but instead of being gone three days we were gone 18. I will give kind of a description of our march as I go along. I wrote in my last letter about Dodge leaving here on an expedition unknown to any of us. well he was gone about 5 days when we got orders to join him at bear creek a distance of about 10 miles from here. (to be continued when I get rested)
Sunday morning
I now take my seat to resume my letter. on the 20th our brigade took up the line of march and on the 22nd we joined General Dodge at bear creek. we

laid there one day waiting for a brigade from Genl. Rosecrans army. The next day we started for Tuscumbia in Alabama. we drove the little squad of rebbels before us without much resistance. I think the main object of our expedition was a blind for another expedition that went out into Georgia to destroy the R.R. between Charleston and Chattanooga. I think we went up in there to draw their attention while the expedition went through. It is a bold undertaking and if accomplished will benefit us a great deal. they were all mounted on mules & carried all their grub on mules calculating to make a quick trip. the Col commanding the expedition says he never expects to get back but if he can accomplish his object he can well afford to lose his little squad. they will be apt to be taken prisoners. The 3rd Ohio is with them. It is a splendid country up in Alla. we did not suffer much for want of meat for we had orders to take any thing we wanted to eat. our co brought in 8 hogs one night besides the beef we drawed of the Les master. Tuscumbia is a nice town but is like all the rest of the towns. all deserted. there is some of the largest springs up there I ever saw. two springs makes a spring as large as Hocking river and it is excellent water. I would like to summer there the best kind. from Tuscumbia we went to a small stream close to Portland. the rebbels destroyed the bridge & planted a battery on the other side but we soon put that out of the way & they skedadeled. we staid there that night & started back the next day. the march went hard with me for we have not marched much lately. I rode the most of the way back. when we were within 15 miles of here they sent out a train of cars to bring in the sore footed lads. I being one of the number to come in on the cars. I commenced to write yesterday for I knew you would want to hear from me but I was too tired to write & I don't feel much like writing today. You spoke about Homers description of the soldiers geting letters. it is indeed a great pleasure for the soldiers to get letters but a good many of them don't like to write them. the fact is we have no good way of writing. I got a letter from aunt Henrietta the other day. she sent me some stamps so I have enough to last me some time. well mother you will have to excuse me for this time also my bad writing for I aint in writing trim today. tell Mattie I will answer her letter when I get a writing streak on me as she had when she wrote to me. no more at present but remain your loving Son, Geo Waterman

S.R. Church

Corinth, Mississippi
May 6th / 63 *

Dear Mother,

It has not been but a few days since I wrote to you but I have received a letter from you since I wrote & as some are going home on furlough I thought I would write a letter & send some money home. The person that I shall send it by lives near Chester & I think it will go safe from there to Pomeroy. It may be that he will be at Pomeroy while he is there. We were paid off yesterday & were mustered again this morning. I would not be surprised if we were paid off again before long. There is no one in this Co. that sends money to Pomeroy & it costs as much to send a small amount as it does a large one & I think it will go safe this way.

I have often said it before but I think I can safely say this time that there is a very fair prospect of us staying here for some time. The whole brigade have turned their teams and ambulances over to the Qt Master. That looks as if we were not going to have much more marching to do. We may have some scouting to do but I think this will be a permanent camp. Some thinks we will be garrisoned here the balance of our time. There is a current report now that we are going to Paducah Ky but I don't credit the report much. I should like very much to summer there. They have commenced to give furloughs now. Three out of a Co. at a time. I don't think I should try to get one. I should like very much to see you all but it would take most four months wages to pay my way there and back. Time is rolling around. The 8th of this month & we have only 14 months to serve then I can go home to stay. There is some talk of us being mounted. If we are I don't care how much we scout around but I don't like to march. You wrote something in your letter that I was going to ask you about & that is if you had kept all the letters that I had written to you. You answered the question before I asked it. I was glad you had kept them. I would keep what I get but I have no good way of keeping them. I did not think I had written so many to you. It will be pleasant to look over them if I ever get home. Then I can explain all about the places that I have referred to in them. It will be quite a memorandum.

It may be some time before you get this for they won't start for a day or two. I shall send $20. Well as I have had quite a task of writing today to all three of you I will bring my letter to an end. Your son Geo.

Sat 9th. We received orders to be ready to march at a minutes notice. We are going by R.R. to Memphis. Whether we will go on any farther than there or not I don't know. We may go to Vicksburg for all I know. If you don't hear from me for a month don't feel uneasy. Them fellas don't go home so I won't send the money in this but will send the first chance I have. Geo.

Pension Letter # 4

Memphis Tenn   May 12th/63 *

Dear Mother,

Your letter of the 4th is at hand & I seat myself to answer it. We left Corinth on the 12th and arrived here on the 19th. We are camped in the suburbs of the town on the south side. We have a beautiful camp as nice a one as we have ever been in. It is on a ridge in a nice shady grove. How long we will stay here it is hard to tell. There was some talk of us going to Vicksburg but I hardly think we will for the brigade that we relieved here went there so I think we will stay here. If it was not for the climate I would as soon be there as anywhere for I don't think there will be much of a fight there. We have had very encouraging reports lately but I don't credit it much.

We have had dispatches that Richmond & Vicksburg was ours but the papers contradict it. Still I think both places will soon fall. I believe Hooker is the man to take Richmond. As a general thing we have good officers in command now & I think a strike in earnest will soon end the war. Grant is a good fighting man but he is too slow. If they give him time & let him alone I believe he will take Vicksburg.

That last letter that I sent I had ready to send by the men that was going home on furloughs but they did not go as we got marching orders so I thought I would send it. If they go I will send the money by them. If we stay here any length of time (& it is the general opinion that they will) the furloughs will be given to the men. I will send it by Frank Worthen who lives near Chester. I think it will be safe to send it that way.

*I had rather be here than at Corinth. It is a good deal nicer place &
everything is cheap to what it is at Corinth. I was very glad to get Lydia's
likeness but I don't think she looks like she used to or it ain't a natural
picture.*

*It was quite a pleasure ride for us to come down here. Rather different way
of moving than we have been in the habit of going. One company out of
this brigade has to go to Corinth every day with the train to guard it. We
stoped at Jackson about an hour but I did not see Will for their camp was
about ½ mile from the depot & I did not dare to leave the train. If our Co
has to go with the train I intend to stop at Jackson & stay till the train
comes back. The regt is there yet but I don't know whether Will is or not he
has not answered my last letter that I wrote about six weeks ago. Well I
must stop for we have not got the camp fixed up yet & I have a poor way
or writing so you must excuse bad writing which is bad indeed. Hoping
these few lines will find you all in as good health as myself. I will close by
signing myself your loving Son Geo. Waterman S.C.*
  Pension Letter #5

Memphis, Tenn
May 20ᵗʰ/63

Dear Mother,
*I seat myself for the pleasant task of answering your letter of the 10ᵗʰ
which I received yesterday. I am in good health & hope this will find you all
the same.*

*There is nothing of much importance going on here now. We have a good
deal of guard duty to do now for the most of the troops have left here since
we came. We have nothing to do but stand guard & a plenty of that. we
have a very nice place here & I think I would sooner be here than at
Corinth.*

*I was a little afraid when we first came here that we would have to go to
Grant. but I don't think we will now unless they send more here. the 3d
brigade was ordered to Vicksburg & they did not want to go so the officers
got up a petition to stay here & got the citizens to sign it. the cowardly
pupps wanted this brigade to go but they could not make the thing work. I*

felt for them but could not reach them (?). this brigade behaved very badly when we came here & the Genl said if we did not behave better than that he would send us where there was some fighting to do. so the boys having no desire to go any farther south cooled down a little.

You said that you had just got the news there that our men had got Richmond. I am afraid that you have been (as we were) sadly disapointed but not discouraged. it is rumored now that our men have got Jackson, Miss but a fellow cant believe it if it is so till six months from now. I believe we have taken Fort Donalson. well if Jackson is ours Vicksburg is too. the taking of Fort Donalson gave us Columbus. the taking of Corinth gave us Memphis & if we get Jackson the result can easily be imagined.

It is the opinion here that it was Halleck's order for Hooker to withdraw across the Rhappahannock & that Hooker wanted to continue the fight. when will the time come when we can have one Genl to command that army. it is my honest opinion that if Hooker had been let alone he would have given Lee a nice whiping if not taken Richmond. Hooker is the man that will take that place if it is ever taken. when we do get a good Genl there, there is always three or four jealous one to work against him. they fight in the east for the name & money not for their country. There was some very bold raids made near Richmond but I am thinking it dont amount to much.

there is going to be a grand celebration here the 6th of June in honor of the fight at this place. it was the 6th of June that we took possession of Memphis. I witnessed the one in honor of the battle of Shiloh & we had a good time & I hope I will have the pleasure of witnessing this one.

I hope we will not be called on to go any farther south this summer not because I dread the fighting for I don't think there will be much of a fight at Vicksburg but it is the climate I dread. it is comfortably warm here but it is a great deal warmer at Vicksburg. the 7th Ohio battery left here the day we came, I did not get to see any of the boys. you know there is a good many from Pomeroy in that battery.

If Aunt & Uncle comes down when you expect them you will get this about the time they are there. if so tell them Arthur & I are well & are doing all we can to put down the rebellion in the way of eating pork beans & hard crackers. Also tell them we answered their last letter.

I have not started my money home yet & I don't know now how I will send it for I don't think there will be any furlough given so I can not send it the way I intended to.

Well I have wrote all I can think of so I will bring my letter to a close by signing my self your loving son

Geo Waterman

S R C

tell the girls they need not be afraid to write to me I wont tell no body no how.

Memphis, Tenn
May 20th/63

Dear Mother,

Enclosed you will find $40.00 I shall send by Frank Worthen. He will put it in the office at Chester. It will go safe from there. I have just wrote a letter today so no more.

Yours in haste. Geo. W.

---

*Memphis TennMay 25th/63 ***

Dear Mother,

Your letter of the 14th is at hand & I seat myself for the pleasant task of answering it. I am enjoying excellent health at present and hope this may find you all the same.

Well the furlough business is in operation now. 30 out of our regt starts home this evening. three out of a Co. I am glad that you are not over anxious for me to get a furlough. I would like the best kind to see you all but when I go home I want to go home to stay. We have only a little more than thirteen months to serve & if I keep my health the time will soon pass off then we can go home to stay at least I hope so but if needs be I will serve three years more but what I will see the end of it. Our Col give the boys quite a lecture before they started. Told them he wanted them to go like men & not drink any liquor while they was gone & show then that soldiers can then be men in the army as well as out. He give them to understand that they must not let copperheads insult them but in all things conduct themselves like men. He talked very good to them.

I think Pa is getting good wages for these hard times but I expect it is hard work. I thought shure Mat would take a school this summer but I expect the milliners trade will pay as well. It is very warm weather here now but we have nothing to do only to stand guard & we have plenty of that. I wrote in my last letter that they were not going to give furloughs & that I would send my money by express. I had just got the letter in the office when the fellow sent word to me that if I wanted to send any thing by him to get it ready. I just merely had time to write a few lines & get it to him. This may get there before that does. He will put it in the office at Chester if he don't go through Pomeroy. If you get this first you will know where the other one comes from.

I think Grant is beginning to do something now. It is reported and generally believed that he has taken Hains Bluff. Took a good many large guns and took the first line of breastworks. Well it is time he was doing something. I suppose old Vallandigham is sent out of our lines. I am glad of that but he had better have been put out of existence. Such men as him is a disgrace to humanity.

Well there is not much to write about as I have to go on guard in the morning & I want to answer Mattie's letter this evening. I ain't much of a hand to compose a letter if there ain't much to write about. I can't write much of a letter however I will write every week if I don't say anything more than I am well. Well no more this time my love to all. Your loving Son Geo. Waterman S.R.C.
Pension Letter # 6

#81

Memphis, Tenn
June 4th/63

Dear Mother,
I seat myself to write a few lines it being some past my usual time writing but I have not received no letter from you this week so I hardly know what to write. Your letter of the 17th of May is the last one I have received. it

has been most two weeks but I put off writing hoping to get one. the mail
has not come in yet today I shall look for one when it comes it.

We have guard duty very heavy here now. we have scarcely any time to
ourselves. hardly time to write our letters. but then I would rather be here
doing guard duty than to be at Vicksburg on the March.

I think very likely if Grant makes another call for troops we will go there.
there has been heavy reinforcements sent to him from here. about all the
troops between here & Corinth have been sent to him. the 18th Ills went
through here the other day & I got to see Will. I did not get to talk with
him only about four hours. he was in good spirits & good health. he said he
had not wrote home for some time & said he was not going to write now till
he knew where he was agoing.

They are bringing a good many prisoners up the river from Vicksburg now.
one Co out of each Regt in our brigade went with a lot to Alton Ill &
before they got back more Co's went. some of them are going to Camp
Chase Ohio. our Co is next on detail so if any more is sent North we will
have to go with them. it will be a gay trip for us & I hope we will have to
go to Ohio with them.

All persons within the lines that wont take the oath are sent south of our
lines & aint allowed to take over $200 worth of property with them. I
was on guard yesterday when they put a family out. I see they don't like it
but they have to take the loss of it. things have been carried on very carless
before we came here. they say our brigade furnishes the best guards that
have ever been here. no citizens passes our lines without being searched.
there is a good deal of smuggling done here. not so much now as there was
before we came here. they stoped a funeral some time ago & opened the
coffin & it was nearly full of quinine & you know that is a scarce article
in the south. when it comes to that you know we have got to be strict with
them no matter how bad they hate it & they do hate it. The women is
awfull saucy but that don't amount to much.

There is nothing new going on here now. everything is quiet now. we used to
be bothered a good deal with bushwhackers but they are played out now
since the Cavalry went out a scouting.

I don't know that I would care much to go to Vicksburg now for we would
never get up to the front unless the army was reorganized then we would
stand a chance of being garrisoned there.

Well I don't know of anything of importance to write so I will close. I will not send this out till the mail comes in & see if I don't get a letter. if it is convenient you may send me some stamps in your next letter.

I intend to send you a present before long but I will not tell now what it is. When I send it I will tell you how I want you to fix it.

hoping this will find you all in as good health as myself I will close

Your loving Son Geo.

The mail has come & shure enough I got a letter. I began to think I had missed one but I see by the number that I did not. I think it is a good plan to number the letters.

I am sorry to hear that Pa is unwell. hope he will soon get well. I will send Lydia's Photograph back only on condition that she will send another. this aint so bad, the more I see it the better I like it.

Tell the girls if I am not mistaken they are all indebted to me for a letter but if they have not time to write I will excuse them.

Well I don't know that I have anything more to write this time so I will stop. My love to you all.

Geo Waterman
S R C

Memphis Tenn June 11/63 *

Dear Mother,

Your letter of the 31ˢᵗ is at hand & I seat myself for the pleasant task of answering it. I am enjoying my usual good health & hope this may find you all the same. Our Co & Co D have been out 6 miles on the R.R. doing guard duty. We were relieved last evening by some cavalry. We had a good time of it for the citizens were so clever to us. They would give us all the milk we wanted & not charge anything for it.

It beats all how they are sending troops down the river. The river is black with troops all the time. Genl Burnsides Corps is now going down. We seem to be the lucky ones this time & I do hope we may continue to be so. I would not wonder if the decisive battle would be fought at Vicksburg. We have been under marching orders since we have been here for Vicksburg but the order has been countermanded. Genl Hurlburt wants to keep us

here if he can but Grant called on him for troops so fast that he came very
near sending us. Now he has sent all the troops he can spare in his
department so I hardly think we will go. Our brigade has several
Companies gone north with prisoners. Two out of our Regt they went to
Ohio and the report is that they are all at home on a ten day furlough. If
that is so they will get to go home free of charge.

You say there has been a dry spell of weather up north. It has been very
dry here for some time past but for a few days we have had plenty of rain.
We are on guard here so often that we can't hardly miss a rain storm.

I approved of the plan of taking boarders if you carry it out but as you
say if it proves a failure it would be a bore to think so many would not
carry it out. Now Mother if you undertake it don't work too much. I
would rather give my wages to hire a girl in your place than to have you
work too hard for I know you can't stand it. I wish I could work it some
way to get along without Pa working too hard for he is getting too old to
work by the days work for a living. I have seen Will, Harvey Pierce &
Frank within the last week.

I suppose you have heard how the Negroes fought at Port Hudson. They
just went for the rebs but they met with a heavy loss. I am glad to hear of
them fighting so well. If it proves to be a good thing we can get a good many
soldiers in a little time for they are plenty down here & if they will do my
fighting I am willing they should do it.

Well I don't know that I have any news to write so I will bring my letter to
an end for I must write one to Mat so as to keep even. No more this time
but remain your loving Son Geo. Waterman. S.R.C.
Government pension letter # 7

#83

Memphis Tenn
June 13th/63

Dear Mother.
I wrote some time ago that I would send you a present. we signed for them
some time ago & they came last evening & I will send mine this morning
so it wont get soiled.

Now I want you to take some of my money that I send home & get a nice frame to put this in & I think it will make a nice picture for the parlor & if I live to get home money cant buy it. it will be nice to look at for years to come.

You will see places in it for the officers Photographs. I don't know whether I can get them or not. they can be put in any time by cutting them places out & pasting the pictures on the back.

I do hope it will go through safe for when they are put in a nice frame they make a very nice picture & whenever you see it you will think of your Soldier boy with the full conviction that he has not forgotten his kind mother.

I don't count this a letter so I wont number it. I see I forgot to number my last but I have it set down. Geo

----

#84

Memphis Tenn
June 16/63

Dear Mother

I received your letter of the 7th this morning & I take this opportunity of answering it for I will be on guard in the morning & I like to answer a letter as soon as I get it especialy them that I get from home for I know it is a great pleasure to you to hear from me often.

I am enjoying excellent health at present & sincerely hope this may find you all the same. I am very sorry to hear of Freddy's poor health this summer. I am afraid he will be sickly through the hot weather. You will have to take good care of him. O how I would like to see the little fellow now.

I received a letter a few days ago from Aunt Laura & Jane. Aunt Laura was at Grand-Pas when she wrote. she said they intended to go to Pomeroy the next week.

I was glad to hear that you had received that money. I dont know when we will be paid off again but I will send all I can home. you said that you hoped we was furnished with food & clothing so I would not have to spend my money for it. we do have plenty to eat such as it is but you know one that has been deprived of the luxuries of life for two years when he sees

something that is fit for a white man to eat his mouth will begin to water &
before he knows it he has his fingers in his pockets & then good bye to the
young green backs. as fer the clothing we can draw all we want of that. we
are allowed so much a year ($42) for our clothing & if we don't draw that
much we are paid for it at the end of the year. I have never drawed my full
amount yet.

It is getting to be very warm weather here now but we have a very nice &
shady camp so we don't feel the heat much. I hardly think we will have any
marching to do this summer. I hope not at least.

There has been a good many troops passing here on their way to
Vicksburg. Grant must be strongly reinforced by this time. we don't hear
anything of much importance from there now. I do hope Grant will succeed
in taking that place for if he does it will be a death blow to the rebbels &
they are sensible of the fact & will be apt to make a strong effort to hold
the place. it has been reported that Johnson has been receiving large
reinforcements but I don't think he has been as strongly reinforced as
reports says he has. Grant is now undermining their forts with the intention
of blowing them up. I hope they will blow them so high that they will never
come down or blow them so low that they will never come up. the later
prefered.

I am well pleased with Lyd's Photograph this time. it is as natural as life a
thousand thanks for it.

Well I will bring my letter to a close as I want to write to Mattie so as to
keep even with her & keep her writing while she is in the notion for she is
the only one of the girls that writes to me. excuse my poor writing for we
have miserable ink at our house. no more at present but remain your ever
loving son.

Geo Waterman
S R C

Memphis, Tenn
June 23d/63

My Dear Mother
Your letter of the 12th was received in due time & read with much

pleasure. I was glad to hear that you were all in tolerable good health. I was afraid that Freddy was going to be sick the most of the summer. I am glad he has got well. I caught a severe cold a few days ago which made me feel unwell for a few days but I am about over it now. it is geting to be very warm here now so much so that I hardly think they will try to march us much this summer. the 5th Ohio & 2d Wis Cavalry went out the other day & engaged the enemy about 30 miles from here & got drove back. we were sent to their assistance but before we got there they were gone as usual. we have no late news of importance from Vicksburg but still think the place will soon fall. I dont think Johnson is going to bother Grant much. I believe Pemberton is holding out there more for spite than anything else for the South & especialy the soldiers thinks he has sold the place. they aint making anything by holding on. Grant is as able to hold out as they are & I know he can get provisions as easy as the rebbels can.

Old Lee thought he would play smash by going into Pa. but his plan was nicely niped in the bud. his object I think was to draw Hookers force out & then he would pitch on to Washington but Hooker was as sharp as he was & did not send any more men than he had.

I dont see why Mr. Pierce don't pay up that note now while he has the money. it would be to his own interest to pay it. I had forgotten all about it till you mentioned it. I think you had better do your best for it. fer my part I aint in any hurry fer it but I think it will be as handy to get at in the bank as in his hands. Harvey was on a study whether to send it home or not. he was afraid Uncle Moses would get it & that would be the last of it. he said that money come hard & he wanted the good of it. I am of his opinion there.

You wanted to know if Will appeared the same as he used to. I did not much more than pass the time of day with him. but as near as I can tell he is about the same as he used to be, I suppose you mean his habits. his looks don't show any signs of bad habits & I had no chance of finding out any other way. Of course he has more of a manly look & way about him & that is all the difference I could see in him.

you seemed puzzled to know what the present was. well if it has had good luck you know before this time. I have no chance to keep the letters that I get or I would, I did think when I first came out that I would keep all I got & did keep them till we got to New Madrid & I had a knapsack full of

*them so I had to throw them or my clothes away & I thought I would burn
them up.*

*our boys that were at home on furloughs got back the other day. they report
good times up north. they say that they dont feel the affects of the war any
up there & that everybody is making money. I am glad to hear of such
good times up there.*

well I have wrote all that I can think of so I will stop.

> *My love to you all, Your Son*
>
> > *Geo*

#86

> *Memphis Tenn*
> *June 29th/63*

*Your letter of the 21st came safe to hand with the morning mail. I was very
glad to hear that you are all well & I am happy to inform you that I am
the same. them two companies that went north with prisoners got back last
evening. they took them to Fort Deleware in Pa. when they were passing
through Pittsburgh some of the Citizens came to the cars & began to
Sympathize with the rebbels & said this was an Abolition war & that the
cause was right & went on that way when some of the boys steped up to
them & told them they could have a free trip to Fort Del. they took them
there & delivered them up as prisoners of war (good) they cant fool with
old soldiers in that way. our boys were treated well in the North. I wish our
Co could make a trip of that kind & I think we will if any more goes
north with prisoners.*

*there is some talk of Johnson withdrawing from Grant & try this place a
rip. it wont be healthy for him to come here. Fort Pickering aint going to be
taken very easy. the breast works are about 20 feet high & mounted with
over 100 siege guns & will hold about 35 or 90 thousand men. I would
consider myself safe inside of the fort. Marmaduke is supposed to be on the
other side of the river but he aint going to do any hurt. We have the report
here that Banks has taken Port Hudson. if that is so Vicksburg will soon
fall. Grant will shurely take Vicksburg but I am afraid we will lose
enough in the east to make up all we gain west. Hooker may be sharp*

enough for them but I am afraid he wont make any thing. I see by the papers that Hooker is on the move. if he and Grant is successful in their present campaign I think it will about wind the things up. God grant that they may & that the war may be brought to a speedy close.

I was glad to hear that you got that Record. I will try to get the officers photographs to put in it.

I was talking the other day with a fellow in this Regt that used to go to school to Uncle Reuben. I asked him what he thought his politics were. he said he thought he was all right but I am of your opinion. I doubt his loyalty & if that is not sound I don't think there is anything sound about him. if he is a butternut I would like to meet him some day just to pay him my compliments in a friendly way, that's so. it is getting to be very warm weather here now & we are having a good deal of rain now.

We will be mustered tomorrow fer two months pay which will be four months due us. I don't know where we will be paid off but I don't think it will be long. I will send 35 or 40 dollars home. I want to have $200 in the bank by the time I get home if I can & I am going to try & make it. If I live to get out of the army I am going to learn to be a Machineist. It is a good trade & one that I like.

tell Lydia she must write to me if she goes up to Grand Pas this summer. I am glad Mattie writes so often to me for I like to get letters from all of you & you all have a better chance to write than I have. so don't none of you wait on me. dont know that I will have time to write to Mat this time but if I don't I will write soon. My love to you all.

Geo Waterman

S R C

#87

Memphis, Tenn

July 6/63

Dear Mother

Your letter of the 28th is at hand & I seat myself to answer it. I am glad to hear that you were all well & I hope this will find you all in as good health as myself. I think by the way you write that we are having a great

deal more rain down here than you have up there. it rains most every day
here now & has for most two weeks. I hope it will rain enough to raise the
Ohio river for I am afraid there will be raids made in Ohio if the river
keeps low.

I see by the last paper that Rosecrans has got Tullahoma & did not meet
with much opposition. I hope he will shove on after them & make them
fight him. reports says that Lee & Meade have had a fight & that Lee got
defeated. it is believed here that Genl Dix will take Richmond now while
Lee is out. I do hope he will. Prentice & Price have had a fight at Hellena
Ark. the rebbels were badly whiped there. 1200 prisoners arrived here last
night from there. the whole army seems to be engaged at present. take it all
through it is the most active time of the war. they are fighting the whole
length of our lines & if this campaign ends in our favor I think the war
will soon end. everything seems to be quiet here at present. we had a very
dry fourth this time. we were kept in camp & not allowed to go to town on
account of so many geting drunk. a good many did get out & went to town
& at night they got in a fuss with the Provost guard & some of the guards
were shot.

There is a good deal of excitement here at present about re-enlistment. they
are to serve three years more & get $400 bounty. they are called the
Veteran Vol. you have perhaps seen the order before this.

If I live to get out of this I will be satisfied with soldiering. not that I am
sick of it at all for I dont know but I would go again when my time is out
& if the war is not likely to be over for I love my country as well as any
body but was not much for a soldier although I have stood it very well so far
& we have seen some hard times if I am any judge of hard times. if I live
to get home it will be a nice thing to talk about if a cold winter night sitting
by a good fire. a good deal nicer than to realize it. a person dont know what
soldiering & fighting is until he realizes it. some will talk about it but they
know nothing.

I suppose you have seen the account of the blowing up of that rebbel Fort
at Vicksburg. if the men had not fought like tigers they would not have
held the Fort. ten Regts went in & held their position against their whole
force till they were reinforced. those western troops fights with a
determination.

You spoke about numbering your letters wrong. I have received that were

147

numbered 8. I have the number of mine set down in my Port-folio & every time I write a letter I set the number down & the date also then I can tell how long since I wrote the last.

Well as I have wrote about all I can think of I will stop by subscribing myself your ever loving Son.

Geo Waterman

S C

#88

Memphis, Tenn
July 12/63

Dear Mother.

Your letter of the 5th is at hand & I seat myself for the pleasant task of answering it. I am well & hope this will find you all the same. it has been very hot here ever since we came here till a few days past & it has been remarkably cold for this time of year. I think by your letter you did not have much of a fourth yourself. for my part if I had been at home I would rather have stayed at home & eaten a good dinner with you & Pa than to went out to the picnic. I hope I can spend the next fourth at home. but that is hard to tell. however we are going on our last year & everything is very encouraging, at present. you have doubtless had the full particulars of the surrender of Vicksburg. it is reported in the morning papers that Port Hudson is taken how true it is we don't know but it is bound to fall soon. You say it is reported there that Memphis is in danger. it was the talk here for a while but it has all died away now & no danger apprehended. there is about a thousand troops here now. we are camped about one mile back from the river & just in the edge of the south side of town. it is thought we will go back to Corinth as soon as we are paid off & I think we will be paid in a week or so. if we go back to Corinth I would not wonder if we done garrison duty the rest of our time. I would rather do that than to be marching so much. there was four out of a Co in our Regt started home yesterday on furlough. Arthur had the offer of going but he did not want to go. I don't know but I would go in the fall if I could get the chance but I don't want to go while it is so hot.

Yesterday we were out on picket & I layed down & took a nap & I dreamed of being at home. I was telling over all I had went through. What I had seen & where we had been. When I waked up I found myself out on picket. I hope the time will soon come when I can be at home & tell over what I have seen & done.

Arthur & I had a talk the other night about that mill. I thought by the way he talked that he never intended I should pay anything toward that mill. so I thought we would have an understanding about it. he said that he intended to pay it all himself & after that he would work his finger nails off but what I should pay for what I had done & what I had paid Lafayette. I told him if he intended to let me out of it we would consider ourselves square but he would not agree to that. he said I should not lose a cent by it but I cant have the heart to take anything for what work I done but if he insists on it I will take what I have paid Laf.

I think I have sent him $55. After this I shall send all my money home that I can spare. Arthur has always used me like a brother & I shall try & do the fair thing with him. he says he don't know but he will try another one if he can ever clear himself of this one. dont know what I will do if I live to get off the army. think I will learn a trade.

I have not heard from Will since he was here. dont know what is the reason he don't write. I don't know where to direct to him or I would write to him. Next time you write tell me how Pa is like to make out with that mill out west. I hope he will come out all right with it. tell Mattie I feel most too stupid to write today so she must excuse me this time. well I have wrote all I can think of this time so I will stop. Your loving Son

Geo Waterman

S R C

Memphis Tenn
July 21st/63

Dear Mother
Your letter of the 13th is at hand & I seat myself to answer it. we have orders to be ready to go to Corinth to guard the train. it is now roll call & I must stop. we have to leave in the morning so I will have to finish when

we come back…Thurs 23d

We have just got back & I now seat myself to finish my letter. we had a very nice trip of it. there was a deserter shot at Corinth today at 8 oclock. the whole division was paraded just as we were leaving. since we left here two Co s of our Regt went out scouting one went to Alton & one went to Vicksburg. we have a good deal of traveling to do lately. I see by the papers that Morgan has been paying the people of Ohio a visit & from all accounts he did not slight the people of Pomeroy much. if they let him get out of Ohio I think they have not got much spunk. the news now from every where is very encourageing. the citizens of this place feel very much down in the mouth about the news lately.

I was very sorry to hear of Lydias poor health. I hope she wont have a very sick spell. I think a trip out in the country would do her good as soon as she is able.

there is a good deal of talk at present about our Regt being mounted & sent across the plains but I think it is like all other reports. every officer in the Regt has signed a petition to go & all of the men are in fer it. I would like to go the best kind if they would mount us. it would be a nice trip & it would take us the rest of our time to go there & back but I dont make any calculation on going. there is 1600 guards to go from here. I hope we will go for it will be a new thing to us & a good deal easier than soldiering & we will see something of the world.

I think the people of Pomeroy must have had quite a jubilee over the news of the fall of Vicksburg. well it is enough to make a fuss about. we now have full possession of the Miss. River & the S.C. is split in twain. I think their cause looks rather hopeless. I am afraid they will soon have to give up their Bonnie Blue Flag.

that what you spoke about Davis sending men to Washington to make a treaty of peace I think started from that delegation that went from La. That state is about ready to come back in to the Union. N. Carolina will be the next. I think that will be the way they will crall back.

I have not much news to write this time for everything is quiet here at present. it is very hot weather now but as a general thing it is healthy among the troops.

I feel tired tonight & as I have not much to write I will stop for it will soon be time for me to write again & if I write too much this time I will have nothing to write the next time. tell Mattie I dont feel like writing tonight so she must excuse me this time.

My love to you all. No more this time but remain your loving Son

Geo

S C

#90

Memphis Tenn
July 28/63

My Dear Mother

Once more the time has rolled round for me to commence my pleasant task of answering your letter which with their usual promptness came safe to hand this morning. We were on picket today & I did not get my letter till we came in this evening. I was very glad to hear that Morgan did not so any more damage at Pomeroy than he did. I saw by the papers that he had been there but it did not say as he done anything. I felt a little uneasy till I heard he had passed there. I knew as long as the gun boats layed there there was no danger. I have seen the benefit of them things. O how many times I have thought how I would like to be there to give him a chase. if our brigade had been well mounted & after him he would get so badly whipped that he never would know where he had been. it makes the old vetern Soldiers mad to think that he went just where he pleased without being captured. when I read your letter where you told about the Soldiers being at our house after water it made me think of the long dreary & dusty marches we have been on & of the times I have stoped at houses for the same purpose but I believe they were better treated. better than we have been treated down here. when we march in to a town down here we have no friends to feed us as they were fed. but they were at home & we are among our enemies. I think the people of Middleport are great military men to run out a battery without any support for it. it is the easiest thing in the world to flank a battery that has no infantry to support it. I would know better than that myself. Pomeroy could be fortified so it could defy the S.C. to take it. It is already naturaly fortified & it is a place that cant be flanked. The Morgan raid is the topic of conversation here at present. he

151

has just been in the part of the county where our Co was got up & the boys are geting letters from there all the time so we have the run of his business. We got a Telegraph this week but it was the 16th & there was not much of Morgan's raid in it. I felt very anxious to get a letter from you so I could hear the news. I feared the excitement if very great would make you sick. I am glad he did not put you to the trouble of moving out.

there has nothing new taken place here since I wrote last. every thing is quiet at present. we had quite exciting times here at the fall of Vicksburg & Port Hudson but you know after a storm there is always a calm. the thing has got to be old so there is nothing new. Charleston seems to be the base of operations at present & we are anxiously waiting to hear of the fall of it. it is rumored in the papers this morning that it is taken but nothing deffinite from there is known. there is where the war begun & I hope it will end there but not til the place is laid in ashes.

You wanted to know if I had heard from Will since he was here. I heard from him once. soon after they got to Vicksburg I got a letter from Frank Lawhead. he just said he saw him & that he was well. that is the last I have heard of him. I dont know where to direct or I would write to him. I told him to write to me when he got there but he did not say as he would or not.

Several of our boys have been to Cairo with prisoners & he has just got back. he brought late Cin papers with him & they contain the official account of the capture of Morgan & all his forces. that is rich indeed & we are all glad to hear of it. I cant help but think that every thing looks favorable for a speedy close of the war. God grant that it may be brought to a speedy close.

tell Pa I have got that knife yet that I got of him the day before I left home also a comb that I brought with me. I shall try to keep them till I go home. Well I don't know that I have anything more to write so I will bring my letter to a close. We have not been paid off yet but expect to be before long. No more at present but remaining your loving Son.

Geo Waterman

#91

Memphis, Tenn
Aug 11/63

My Dear Mother: Your letter of the 2d came safe to hand with this morning mail & I avail myself of this opportunity of answering it. I have as I stated in Mattie's letter been rather under the weather but have been geting better for a few days past so I am doing duty now. I am troubled with the diarrhea a good deal this summer especialy in hot weather, it keeps me weak all the time so I dont feel like myself half of the time, some times I will feel very well for a few weeks till I eat something that will start the diarrhea started again. I am very careful what I eat in fact we have no chance to get any fruit or green stuff for there aint two men in the Co. that has a cent of money, I haven't had any for a long time. We are all very anxious to get paid off but there aint much signs of the Paymaster at present. there is most six months pay due us now but I dont expect we will get but four months pay if we are paid very soon.

You said you should think it would be tiresome to stay in camp so long. I assure you it is & as you say, the same thing every day over & over but well knowing as we do what marching is we are very well satisfied to remain in camp. If we live to see eleven months roll around we will be free men once more & the time will soon wear away. We will not see more than five or six months more of active servis, I would not be surprised if we would remain here till winter for Genl Hulburt has resigned & they say Prentiss has command here now, if so he will be apt to keep us here for we were under him in Mo. & he thought a good deal of this Regt. and as we are good at garrison duty we will be apt to remain here for sometime yet, it may be we will take a part in the fall campaign but I am of your opinion about the fighting in this department, I think it is about at an end. Charleston & Mobile is the two main points now & Charleston is bound to fall & that soon too. Grant is now making preparations to send his army round to Mobile by way of N. Orleans, I think I would like the trip in the fall.

I guess there is nothing of that expedition going to Utah that I wrote about time ago. The excitement has all died away & nothing is said about it. I dont know what it was for or where it was going & I guess nobody els did, the officers got up a paper of some kind & all signed it. we have since heard that it was for us not to be paid while we stay here on account of the men getting drunk when they have money, if that is so they had better not let the men know of it. I was glad to hear that you had heard from Will. I did not know where he was. I will write to him before long & see if I can get on his track again, sometimes I will write to him and will get a letter or two from him & that is the last I will hear from him for a long time. I was surprised to hear that Gust (Aust) Hudson had enlisted again, he ranks me a little now. If I ever enlist again it will be in Cavalry, they have more to do than Infantry but there marching aint so hard. well I dont know that I have anything more to write of importance so I had better quit. hoping this will find you all enjoying health & happiness I close by subscribing my self your Ever loving Son

Geo. Waterman

S.R. Church

Please send me some stamps as I have but one left & am out of chinck.

#92

Memphis, Tenn

Aug 16/63

My Dear Mother,
Your letter of the 9th came safe to hand this morning. it was the only letter for the co but what gave me the most pleasure was the arrival of Mr. French with that package. Dear Mother it would be useless for me to try to describe the pleasure it gave me to receive that present, it is just such a thing as I needed & wanted & then to think of its coming right from home & being so plentifully supplied with everything that I needed. I was indeed very much delighted to get it & I most heartily thank you for it, you may expect to see that again if I live to get home I have a comb & a knife that I brought from home & I have carried them all the time I have been out & am going to try & take them home with me if I ever go home again & God grant that I may & soon too, you know I promised to bring Freddy a present when I went home. I wish you would tell me what would be the most likely to please him so if I can get it I will know what to get very likely he

has forgotten all about it by this time.

I think I wrote in my last about being unwell I don't know that I am any better or worse than I was then, I don't do any duty now nor I aint going to till I feel like it, I have done duty when I feel like it, I have done duty when I felt worse than I do now, but I have concluded it don't pay, we have the best Dr now we have ever had. if a man is sick he wont tell him go on duty. I told him I had the chronic diarrhea & how long I had had it & he told me he could cure it for me but it would take time & I must not do any duty for the present. I went to him 4 days some time ago till I began to feel better & then I commenced to do duty & it got worse on me, he told me I quit off too quick. now I have made up my mind not to do any hard duty as long as I am in the servis till I feel better than I do now. I have went on marches when I have felt as every step was my last but I have swore off now, I could do duty if I was so minded but I aint. I don't want you to feel uneasy about me for I have told just how I feel, there is nothing the matter of me but the chronic diarrhea but that aint very easy to stop in the army. well it is roll call & I must stop for tonight, I will finish tomorrow & write some to Mat.

Monday 17th

I will now finish while it is cool, when it is hot it is very uncomfortable in the tents, we had a little rain last night & it is quite comfortable this morning. the co is out on picket & I have the tent all to myself. two of our boys start home this morning on a thirty day furlough, the first got 20 the next 25 & this time they get 30 days, I don't know but I would take one if they would offer me one but I wont ask them for one for my time will soon be out & then I can go when & where I please.

You did not say in your last letter or two whether Pa had employment now or whether you had given up taking any boarders. I am glad that the girls are willing to take hold & do the hard work when they see that you are not able to do it, it is no more than right that they should do it now after you have got so you cant stand hard work. you spoke about sending your Photograph to me. I would be very glad indeed to have it & have often thought of asking you for it if you can get a Photograph I would like to have it but I have no good way to carry a picture in a case & it is apt to get broke, them stamps came in good play for I was just out. I wrote a letter to Will the other day & sent the last one I had. If that money I sent home

155

to buy stamps with is gone you may take some out of the next I send home
for I dont want you to spend any money for that purpose, are you like to get
that money that B R Pierce owes you; I wish he would pay it & I think
now is as good a chance as he will have to pay it soon for I dont believe
Harvey will send any more soon.

Well I believe I will close & write some to Mat. hoping this will find you
all well I sign my self your ever loving Son Geo Waterman

S.R.C.

#93

Memphis Tenn.
Aug 27th/63

My Dear Mother:

this being my regular day for writing I thought I would commence thinking
I would get a letter from you this morning but I was disappointed. I think I
will get one in the morning & I will have this ready to send out by the
morning mail.

I have changed my base of operations since I wrote last. being tired of
camp life & not liking the Hospital I have taken up my abode at a private
house. it is a widow woman that lives here (two of them) & they are afraid
of the Soldiers & wanted a guard to stay here and they board him. the Dr
thought it would be the best thing he could do for me so he sent me out here
thinking a change of diet would be good for me & I think it will too for I
get good grub here & begin to feel better they are very kind people here & I
have nothing to do but fight mosquitoes of a night. I dont know but I will
get homesick if I stay here long. it seems more like home than any place I
have been since I left home but still it aint home. I dont know but I will try
for a furlough if they give any more but I think it is doubtfull if they give
any more or not for I would not wonder if our brigade was sent over in
Ark. there is some talk of it now. they can go where they please but I don't
intend to do much more marching. it still continues hot here yet but today is
a very nice cool day with the appearance of rain. it is a day that a fellow
could enjoy him self if he was well. if I am a little unwell in body my
spirits is still up & I never allow myself to get the blues. I take every thing

as it comes (even my medicine) & make the best of it. Ambition will carry a fellow a good way & I believe that is half that has made me hold out as well as I have since I have been out. I will admit I have been favored some by the officers but I have done duty when if I had been at home I would have thought I was sick. I congratulate myself on my good luck now for I have got in a good place & exempt from all duty & at perfect liberty to go where I please. in fact I am a free man at present & the world goes well with me now. I have a room to my self where I can collect my thoughts long enough to write a letter which is hard to do in camp. It seems odd to me to be at a house after liveing in camp so long. it brings to my mind a faith recollection of times before I left home to be a soldier boy. O, that the time may soon come when we can all return to our homes to dwell in peace & dream no more of war. some times I think the day is not far distant when the South will be convinced of their folly & will be willing to throw down their arms & return to the Union. two more such blows as Vicksburg & Port Hudson will open their eyes & them two places will be Charleston & Mobile, their sentence is pronounced & the time for execution is close at hand we are daily expecting to hear of the fall of Charleston. at least accounts we have one gun with in range of the city & was throwing shell in the town which soon brought out a flag of truce but for what purpose was not stated. it also said that they were moveing the guns out of Fort Sumpter. our guns is makeing the brick & mortar fly every pop. there is where the war began & how glad I would be if it would end there. if I was shure the war would end with the fall of Sumpter I would soon begin to think of seeing home. everything looks favorable as far as I can see. the papers speaks a good lately about N. Carolina trying to crall back in the Union. hope she will. all they want now is for one state to make a brake & the rest will soon follow just like a flock of sheep. I honestly believe there is a Union feeling growing in N.C. & I think the North ought to encourage it & get the state back. we brought Mo out all right & I believe the people enjoys them selves full as well so if they were under Jeff's control. Uncle Sam is a good Uncle to all as long as they will obey him.

Who do you think I saw yesterday. one of my school mates, Melvill Dudrey. I did not know him at first but soon recognized him & was glad to see him. aint it strange how friends will meet & at times when they least expect it. well I declare if I aint in a writing humor today. however I will go on as long as I can find paper.

I have nothing els to do & I might as well write ahead for if you are like me you will be glad to get a long letter once & a while. I will give you a little description of the people here. like all other cities there is two classes. these folks that I am with I think counts themselves in with the A No 1 class. I am not much acquainted with them yet but I judge by their eating hours; breakfast at ½ past 8 o'clock dinner at two and supper at 8 in the evening whether they think they out-rank a soldier or not I don't know but they give me a table all to myself. odd as it looks it just suits me. I will put up with most any thing for the sake of getting good grub & I get that here. I am afraid if they let me stay here till I get well I will be a long time at it. one good thing. there is no girls here to bother me. for of all plagues they are the worst. well here I am writing just whatever comes in my mind but you must excuse me for I am about half asleep. I took some pills this morning that had some opium in them or laudinum or something that makes me feel sleepy but I think they help me. we have a very good Dr. now, one that is good to the men & dont feel above his business because he can wear red tape.

Mell Dudrey said he saw Will a few days before he left Vicksburg. he was well. I wrote a letter to him some time ago but have received no answer yet. Well I guess I will stop for the present. if I get a letter in the morning I will write some more & if not I will let it go at this. dont feel uneasy about your soldier boy for he is all right. & sincerely hopes this will find you all in good health.

Your son Geo

Waterman

S.R. Church

#94

Memphis, Tenn
Sept. 7/63

Dear Mother

this pleasant day finds me seated in my little room trying to pen a few lines to you to let you know how I am. I am a good deal better than I was when

I wrote last, am gaining very fast now. I think if I take good care of myself I will soon get well. I have got the diarrhea about stoped on me now but if it come on again I will try your medicine. I am looking for some of the boys over with a letter for me for today is my mail day. I thought I would commence my letter so if any of the boys came over I could send this back I don't run around much for I feel better to keep still. I get very lonesome here some days but it is so much better for me to stay here so I try to content my self. these folks here are so proud that they cant talk to a common man so I have no company at all but they feed me mighty well & that is all I came for. we have chicken most every day & no body but a soldier knows how to eat chicken. these folks are about to sell out & leave & I don't know whether I will get to stay any longer or not. there aint no need of a guard here but I am willing to stay for I like this kind of soldiering I am so nervous this morning that I cant half write so I will quit a while.

Tuesday 8th

after I stopped writing yesterday I took a notion to go over to camp. I got over there & stayed till most night. I thought there would be a letter for me but there was none. The boys said if one came today they would bring it over. Benj French was over here the other day & we got to talking about home & I do believe I got home sick I dont want to go till I can go to stay but if I aint able for duty when we are ordered away from here I believe I will try for a sick furlough & if I ever get home I will stay till I am well. Well I have just eat my breakfast & have been up more than four hours. I find that city life is different than camp life. in camp we eat just when we get hungry. if I stay here long it will spoil me for soldiering. the boys wont claim me any more in the co. when I went over to camp yesterday they wanted to know what city fop that was coming. do you hear from Will any more. he wont write to me. I wrote a letter to him about four weeks ago & have not received no answer yet — perhaps he did not get it. I directed it to Vicksburg. just ten months from today if I live I will be a free man. on the 8th of next July we will be homeward bound. if we have as easy times for the next nine months to come as we have had in the last nine months time will soon pass off. we have been in this place 4 months & it dont seem but a few days. there is still some talk of us going over in Ark. but it is all among the boys the officers dont say anything about it. still I would not wonder if we went if they send any more troops over there. We have been in camp so long that I would not wonder if they sent us out before long. well I have just received your letter of the 30th & one from Mattie. I was very glad to get them you said you forgot to send me a darn needle but you are slightly mistaken for there was one in the package. you call it a package of trifles. be it so I value them very highly & will try to keep them. you wanted me to write just how I am. I assure you I have wrote just how I felt. I would not for the world deceive you in the least. I am glad to hear that you have your health better lately. I will write as often as I can & let you know how I am geting . My mail carrier is waiting to take this back with him so you must excuse me this time & I will write more the next tell Mat I haven't time to write to her this time no more this time from your Son Geo Waterman

S C

#95

Memphis, Tenn
Sept 12th, 1863

Dear Mother.

I received a letter from you rather unexpected it being two days ahead of the regular time still I was as glad to get it as though I had been looking for it. I see by your letter you are anxious for me to get a furlough & go home. I have been thinking some of it lately but have not applied for one & I don't know whether I could get one if I should try, since I received your letter I have been thinking about it & I believe I will ask the Capt & if he wont give me one I will speak to the Dr for a sick furlough & if that fails it is all I can do so if I do fail you must not be disapointed. I will not for I don't expect I could get one. I don't want you to feel uneasy about me (but I am afraid you do) for I think I will be well in course of time. I am gaining but it is slow. it is as you say I let it run too long & it will take time to cure it. that is what the Dr told me when I first went to him but he said he could cure me in time & I think he will. I am not discouraged as long as I

160

can keep on my feet. I will not do any duty as long as I am unwell. be assured if I cant get a furlough I will take good care of myself & try to get well.

I feel in very good spirits this afternoon on account of the good news received. we hear that Rosecrans occupies Chattanooga also that our forces is in possession of Morris Is. with battery Wagner & Gregg. if that is so look out for Charleston for it is bound to fall these folks here be it known are secesh & they don't feel quite as gay over the news as I do. so the less they believe of it the better for them & in fact they wont believe it. the state of Tenn is now clear of the rebbels & I would not wonder if she soon applied for her old seat in the Union. the first of next month old Parson Brownlow is going to start his paper called the Knoxville Whig & Rebble Ventilator. I would give a dollar to see the first paper. at last accounts the rebbels were retreating in Ark. very doubtful if they stand much of a fight. I think upon the whole the "S C" is about played out.

In the Telegraph of Sept 3d you will see a speech our Col made. I have often wondered why he never made a speech in the army for he is a very popular man but I see in his speech that he said he had not made a speech while he was in the army nor did not intend to. he is a very inteligent & well informed man & a good military officer.

they are not likely to need any reinforcements in Ark so I see no probability of us leaving here soon. we have drawed new guns again, they wanted the rifles we had for mounted infantry for they were a short gun & handier to handle on horse back. I think there will be a good deal of Infantry mounted this fall. there was a report that we were to be mounted but it was all talk. we can march most as fast as cavalry so they will never mount us, except by knapsacks.

well as I want to write some to Mat I will have to wind this up. I am going to go over to camp in the morning & I want to take this to the office. hoping this will find you all in the enjoyment of health. I will close by signing myself as ever your loving Son

Geo Waterman

S R C

P.S. In my letter of the 1st of this month I sent a receipt for $20. if you get it let me know.

Geo

#96

Memphis, Tenn
Sept 19, 63

My Dear Mother
I will look for a letter from you tomorrow & I thought I might commence
& write some today & finish to-morrow or when I receive one from you. I
don't want my letter to be a day behind if I can help it for I know you will
be anxious to hear from me as often as possible. I had a chill yesterday & I
feel rather stupid this morning & I have a slight head ache. other ways I
feel very well. I have not been bothered much with the diarrhea for the last
week & I think I can cure it in course of time. I have gained some in flesh
but not much in strength for I have a very poor appetite & cant yet relish
anything so, you know I would gain very slow still I have a better appetite
than I had two weeks ago. well according to your request I have applied for
a furlough and I must confess I succeeded better than I expected but I aint
certain of it yet. I first went to the Dr & he promised to see that my name
was sent in if any more went. I then spoke to the Capt. & he promised me
also but I would not give much for the promise but if the Dr takes it in
hand I may get one. you must not be disappointed if I don't get one for I
am no way dangerous & I think I will get well some time if I have to stay
here. it will be a week at least before we would start if there is any more
furloughs given. the last that went have not all got back yet and they wont
start any more till they return. as soon as I find out for certain I will write
& let you know.
Sat morning 19th. well I feel a good deal better this morning. I had another
chill yesterday after I quit writing other ways I feel very well & this
morning I feel better than common & I don't think I will have any today
but I cant tell yet. the Dr is giving me quinine & it makes my head feel
bad. I feel about half asleep all the time. I will stop until I receive your
letter which I am looking for today. if any comes some of the boys will
bring it over to me… Well here it is Sunday morning & my letter is not
finished yet but it is because I did not receive one yesterday. if none comes
today I will send this out any how so it wont be behind times. well I missed

the chills yesterday & this morning I feel better than I have for a week or more. if I get the chills broke I will get along fine for the diarrhea has not bothered me much for a week or more & I feel very much in hopes I will soon get well. there was some talk of us leaving here sometime ago & in fact we had marching orders about a week ago & I think it was the intention for us to go to Little Rock Ark for when that place was evacuated our orders was counter-manded & it is the general opinion that we will stay here some time yet. if we stay here much longer we will be apt to remain all winter the battery that belongs to our brigade has orders to build stables & that looks like staying a while. but there is no telling... I received a letter from Mat the other day, it was mailed at Athens, her & Aunt & Uncle was up to Athens & she mailed it there. I received one from Lydia Jane & Lewis since I wrote last. Lydia writes that she is contented & is getting fat as a fig.. well Arthur has just come over but no letter so I will finish this & send it back by him as I want it to go out today. about all of the furloughed men have got back now & it wont be but a few days till I can tell who will go next time. if I don't succeed in getting one you must not be disappointed nor feel uneasy about me for I am doing fine at present. if I should soon get well I don't want to go home. well I don't know as I have any thing more to write so I will bring my letter to a close. hoping this will find you all in the enjoyment of health & happiness I remain as ever your loving son. Geo Waterman

SRC

#97

Memphis, Tenn
Sept 23/63

My Dear Mother:
It has not been but a few days since I wrote to you but I had received no letter from you this week when I wrote, this morning I received one it being four days behind time. I know by the way you write you are worrying about me & I am sorry for it but I know you cant help it. you are so anxious for me to come home that you are looking for me. I wrote in my last that the

prospect was very encouraging for me going home. well before the boys all got back that had gone we got marching orders & they aint going to give any more furloughs till they see whether we move or not. if we don't they will be apt to give more & if we do have them that are sick will be apt to be sent to the General Hospital & if I get there I will stand a good chance to get a sick furlough & it will be the first thing I will try for, we aint certain of moving yet nor I aint certain of what they will do with the sick but that is what they generally do with them. I have got the chills entirely broke now & I am getting better other ways. the chills set me back a little but I have gained that all back & am doing fine now & begin to have a little better appetite than I had. about a person haveing a craving appetite when they have this disease is a mistake with me at least for I have not had scarcely any appetite while I have been sick. cant eat enough for my own good let alone eating enough to hurt me. about all I can eat is bread butter & milk & you know I cant eat enough of that to hurt me you wanted me to come home while I was able. perhaps you think I am getting worse. not so. I am gaining slowly & I honestly believe I aint sick enough to get a sick furlough but if I could get one & get home perhaps I could get it lengthened by a Dr there for I have no doubt when I got on the river the change of water would give me a back set. I will do all I can to get one & I think I can some time this fall. if I should get in the General Hospital & cant get to go home I am going to try to get to be waiter & then I can stay there as long as I please & it will be easier than soldiering for there will be very active times this fall & we may have to take a part in the fall campaign & I cant stand it to march now so if I have a chance to get detailed as waiter in the Hospital I will have easy times, I have such a nice place here that I hate to have them leave for I would have to leave too. I have a chance to stay here as long as we stay here or till I get well & I have no duty to do here & a good warm room to stay in. I have nice times all to myself. I wrote a letter to Mattie yesterday but I don't know whether she will be there when it gets there. I received a letter from Aunt H this morning they were all well. she writes for me to go home if I can. well as it has been such a short time since I wrote to you I have not much to write this time. the fellow that brought my letter over this morning said he would be over again this afternoon & I will send this back by him. I will tell you the four that belong to my mess beside myself A. Lawrence EA Conant WJ Hamilton & Saml Jennings.

You will see on that record.. we are all about of a size & a civil set of boys, some of them is over here most every day. Conant is coming over this afternoon & bring over the two last telegraphs. Arthur comes over as often as he can. he is about the same as a brother to me & I will hate it if we have to part but we cant always be together. Well I will have to draw my letter to a close. don't worry about me for I am doing fine. hopeing this will find you all in good health I remain as ever

Your loving son Geo Waterman

S R C

Memphis Tennessee Sept 27th/63 *

My Dear Mother,

I received your letter of the 18th this morning. I went over to the Co & when I got there I found Wm Mc and Homer Waterman. You better believe I was glad to see them. Well I am happy to inform you that I am a good deal better than I was when I wrote last. I feel in hopes now that I will soon get well. The probability is now that we will leave here in a very few days. I will not be able to march now I don't intend to try but if I am left behind I will be able to take care of myself now. We are going to join Rosecrans & we will go as far as Iuka on the cars & march through from there. It will be a hard march and them that can't march will be apt to be left here or Iuka. They may take the convalescents like me clear through but I don't think they will. It may be that you will not get my next letter at the regular time if we are moving I will have a poor chance to write if I go with them so you must not feel uneasy. I will write as often as I can & let you know how things is working.

I am sorry you missed that letter for I know you must have felt uneasy about me. I think it very strange I can't send anything in a letter and have it go through. That is the first letter than has missed since that one I sent $10 in at Corinth. They won't get no money and any more of my letters. The loss of that receipt is no difference you can draw the money & receipt for it as well for the Co treasurer knows that there is $20 for you. That letter was wrote soon after we were paid off & I suppose some one thought they would get some money. Wonder if they did.

165

You wrote to me in regard to the way we were sworn in the service. Three years or sooner discharged is the way we were sworn in & when over three years is up we are out & a going home. Which will be over nine months now. I don't know how it is about them that was sworn in for three years as during the war. I don't think there was many sworn in that way. They are giving $402 bounty to all three years men that have less than a year to serve for reenlistment. I think I will serve my time out here before I go again. You say for me to do as I think best about getting a furlough. Well if I am like to get well soon I don't want to go till my time is out but as you say if I get worse again I will try to go home. I am perfectly satisfied when I am well. I think I will get along now it is coming cool weather. I don't like the idea of leaving here for I have such a nice place to stay. There has been some very hard fighting between Rosecrans & Bragg & not much made on either side but I think it is about over with for the present. Burnsides will be apt to have some fighting to do now. It will be two weeks before we will get with Rosecrans & he will either whip us or get whipped by that time. They are repairing the Memphis & Charleston R.R. it may be we will be posted along the R.R. but it is the general opinion we will join Rosecrans.

The whole 16th army corps (Genl Hurlburt) is under marching orders & the 15th Shermans is coming here. The 4th Va. belongs to that & Wm. & Homer is going to wait here till they come up. I would like to see the 4th for I know a good many of them. I am glad Will writes home once in a while for that is the only way I can hear from him. They did not have any fight at Little Rock. I recon the post master will think I am drunk for writing so much won't he. This is three letters in the last eight days. Well I have wrote all I can think of so I will close. My love to all. This from your loving Son Geo.

*Government pension letter# 8

166

#99

Memphis, Tenn
October 5th / 63

Dear Mother
You will no doubt think by the way I wrote the last time that by this time
we are way up in the mountains but we aint & I find myself on the very
spot that I was when I wrote before. it is very uncertain whether we will
move at present. the troops that were to take our place here are going right
on through as fast as they come up. I am still crawling up but not as fast as
I was when I wrote last. the reason is this woman is packing up to leave &
she got me to help her & I stirred around too much & it rather throwed
me off the hinges for a day or two. I saw that I was doing more than I was
able so I played quits on her & I begin to feel better. she will leave today or
tomorrow & I expect I will have to go back to camp unless this other
woman wants me to stay here. if I have to go back to camp I believe I will
stay at the Hospital for it will be better for me, well I have just had a talk
with the woman that is going to move in here & she wants me to stay so
that is a settled fact.
I have not received no letter from you this week yet but I am looking for
Arthur over every minute with a letter for me for this is the day for me to
get one. the 24th Va is here now & it seemed almost like going home to see
so many of the boys that I knew. you cant imagine how glad I was to see so
many right from home. they were all in good health. Lyman White says he
is about as well as ever. Jim Davis is home on a furlough. Well one of the
boys has come over but no letter for me. the river is so low that the boats
cant hardly run. I know you have written but the letter has been delayed
some way, it is getting tolerable cool weather now for the time of year. we
have had two or three frosts here lately. Well this fellow is waiting to take
this letter over to camp so I cant write much more & in fact I have wrote
about all you will want to know. that is how & where I am. as for news
there is none. I am most ashamed to send this small letter but I will write
again the last of this week if I get a letter from you. tell the girls that Will
Mc & White sends their compliments to them. I got a letter from Will the
other day he is at Little Rock Ark he says he is down there on hunt of
bears & other small game. Well I must stop for Sam wants to go back. My

love to you all. Your Soldier boy Geo.

S.C.

#100

Memphis, Tenn
Sunday Oct 11th/63

Dear Mother
Again I seat myself for the pleasant task of writing you a few lines. it is just two weeks today since I have had a letter from you still I don't think it any fault of yours for we don't get mail regular now while the river is so low. I don't intend to mail this till tomorrow but I thought I would write some today as I have nothing els to do. I am a good deal better than I was when I wrote last. I am gaining very fast now. I had the chills a day or two before I wrote last but was getting better when I wrote & I have been getting better ever since. If I don't have the chills any more I think I will soon get well for I feel more like myself now than I have for sometime. the woman that was here when I came here has left & another family moved in. I am very well suited with the change for now I am treated like a white man & before I ranked between a white man & a negro. how long I can get to stay here is more than I can tell. if I keep on gaining I will soon be able for duty & I expect I will have to go back to the Co. then. well you will see by the heading of my letter that we are in the same old place yet & have not made that intended move than I wrote so much about nor can I see any sign of making it now but I have come to the conclusion that I don't know anything about what we are going to do so I don't think it best for me to say much about it still every man has a right to think & I think if we don't leave here we will stay here & that is about as near as I can come to it & I believe I will hit nearer the mark this time than I did before, in fact soldiers aint supposed to know any thing but they have the privilege of thinking so you must not take what I write for the truth but for what I think. I think from all appearances we will winter here that is if we don't leave. but I aint going to say what we will do for I don't know, the 55th OVI has been here & I had a two days visit with Harvey Pierce and

Frank Lawhead. I have seen a good many of my old acquaintances lately. Arthur came over the other day with that scrap Book. he told me he had brought over a book for me to read. didnt tell me how he got it. I took the book & looked at it & saw it was a Patent office report & it poped into my head right off that it come from home but I thought it impossible. I asked the boys where they got it. they would say over in camp. I looked all through the book to find some name & finely run on to a piece of paper that explained it. I heartily thank you for the present for I can spend my idle hours very pleasantly reading it. I cannot describe my thoughts after the boys had left & I was alone & got to thinking of the many hours you spent in fixing the book for me & perhaps thinking all the time of your absent soldier boy. it was enough to assure me that I am not forgotten by my dear Mother & I hope my letters gives you the same assurance for that is all I have to send you & if they aint good in quality the quantity will make it up. as much as I think of your present I cant promise to keep it till I go home unless we should be in camp all the time for when we are on a march I never load myself heavier than I can help. I did not see the fellow that brought the book though but I think it was Jim Davis. Next Tuesday is Election day & I will put in my first vote but old Val won't get it. there aint many in our Regt will vote for him & no person but a traitor will vote for him. I am so glad the Soldier has the privilege of voting. I am thinking if it was left to the Citizens old Val would stand a chance. but as it is he cant come in. it would be an everlasting disgrace on the state if he was elected & I would never own that I was ever a citizen of Ohio. I would sooner vote for Jeff Davis & it would not be any more of a disgrace to the state if he was Governor. still I don't think there is much danger of either of them being elected. Well I will close till after the mail comes in & if I get a letter I write some more & if not I will send this out for I don't want it to be behind times.

Your son,
Geo Waterman SRC

Memphis, Tenn Oct 17th/63*

Dear Mother,

In haste I seat myself to write you a few lines to let you know that we are going to leave here. The Col just passed here & told me to report over to the Regt for we were going to leave in the morning but I can't tell where we are going. I am still getting better but not able to march but I expect I will go along if I do I won't carry anything & will perhaps ride. Well the Dr has just been here & he said that the sick would go on the cars so I will not have to march. We are going to Corinth from here & I don't know where we will go from there but I will let you know as soon as possible all that is going on. We will be paid off this afternoon & I will send all of my wages home this time. I have a plenty of my last pay to do me.

I hate to leave my little house but I will have to do it. I have been here almost two months. It will be three weeks tomorrow since I have had a letter from you. I don't know what is the reason of it. That one that Will Mc brought through is the last one I have got. I begin to feel anxious to hear from you. Well I must pack up and go over to camp. If I can find out anything more about the move I will write some more & if not I will send this so no more this time.

Your Son Geo. Waterman S.R.C.

Governments pension letter # 9

On board the Steamer Rob Roy Nov 10th/63*

Dear Mother,

I seat myself to write you a few lines to let you know that I am still alive. I expect you begin to feel uneasy about me by this time for it has been about two weeks since I have wrote. The reason is because there has been no chance to send out mail. The last time I wrote was at Bunnsville from there we went to Iuka & stayed three days & our brigade was transferred into Sherman's Corps (15_) & they are marching through to Chattanooga & the convalescents are going around by the way of Louisville or Nashville. I don't know which way it is the intention to leave all that is not able for duty *at some hospital. I think very likely I will be left but I can't tell. If I have to be moving around all the time I will not be able for duty this winter. I ain't quite as well as I was when I wrote before for we have been moving around all the time. I think the Dr intends to leave me behind for he knows I won't be good for anything this winter & yesterday he took my name in full & the co I belong to so I think he is going to leave me behind. If he does it is good bye soldiering for I will never go back to the Regt again if I can get on a detail of any kind at the hospital.*

I have a very poor chance to write and not very much time for we will soon be to Paducah & then we will have to change boats. It has been so long since I have wrote that I thought I would write a few lines & send the first chance. I will write a good long letter when I get where I can tell all about this trip for it is very interesting. At present I have not time. At Paducah we will take a boat for Louisville or go up the Cumberland to Nashville. I will write again the first opportunity. Direct your letters the same & if I don't go back to the regt Arthur will remail them & send them to me till I tell you where to direct. Don't feel uneasy about me for I will get along well. Dr. Smith has always treated me well & I think I can get to put-up at some northern hospital this winter. I shall try for it anyhow. Well for the present I will close. Excuse bad writing for the boat shakes so I can't write. Hoping this will find you all well. I remain your loving Son Geo. Waterman S.R.C.

P.S. For fear you do not get that other letter I will mention in this that I expressed $30 with Arthur & it is in Edward Lawrences's care.

*Government pension letter # 10

- -

Nov. 12th/63 Paducah, Ky.*

As I have no chance of sending my letter out I thought I would write some more &let you know when I have got to now. I have at last got my wish. That is get in a good hospital. We arrived here on the 10th & the morning of the 11th them that was not able for duty was sent to the hospital. We have most an excellent place to stay. I have as good a bed to sleep in as you could give me if I was at home. Everything is clean and nice. The sight of it is enough to make a man well. I feel a good deal better than I did when we were on the boat. I expect I will be here the most of the winter for they never send us men away from the general hospital tell he is sound and well. I don't think I will be good for anything until spring. I am looking forward to next duty then I am going home. It won't be long 8 months will soon roll away.

Well I don't know that I will have anything more to write. I will write again soon. Direct to hospital No 2 Paducah Ky. Write soon for I have not had a letter from home for three weeks. I don't expect any more till I get an answer to this so you will know where I am.

Your Son Geo. Waterman

*Government pension letter # 11

(Letter from Sophronia to George)

Pomeroy, November 14, 63

My dear George,
As it is the regular day for writing, I now avail myself of this opportunity to write a few lines to my dear absent soldier boy. It has been almost three weeks since I had the last letter & it seems a very long time to me. I think you must have written as it did not reach here, or else you have not had a chance to write for I do not think that you are to blame for it no indeed. You have been such a good boy to write that I cannot lay the blame to you but it really does seem a very long time since I have heard from you, I am very anxious to know where you are & how you are getting along by this time. I often ask myself this question, will he ever come home again but it remains unanswered, & will until time reveals it to us. I have to await with patience the measured track of time. & you my dear boy no doubt, are as impatient for the time to come as I am, the lord grant that your previous life may be spared to see that time. & I can live to welcome you home again. Most every body think that the war will soon end, & I hope it will, for there has been too many lives lost already. It has made a great many widows & orphans, it has made very hard times for a great many

poor people, & the most of them are women and children.

Prices for almost everything are higher than I ever knew them to be here. Wheat & flour is about the same that it was before the war, but corn has been double all summer. I don't know what it is now, but I think it is some less. Potatoes 1 doll beans 2 dolls. Butter 23 cts, fresh pork 8 cts per pound tea 1.60 per lb. coffee 37 to 41, sugar 15 & 16 cts pound: hay 25 & 30 dolls per ton, and straw is now selling for 10 dollars a ton & oats for 50 & 60 per bushel.

All kinds of cloth sells very high. Cotton cloth that used to sell for 10 cts per yrd. Now sells for 37 & 40 & all kinds of cotton goods accordingly, common hommade jeans is a dollar & a quarter per yard. for cotton yarn is 5 dolls a bunch, now you may see that it is hard for poor folks to clothe a family when all kinds of cloth is so high, calico is 25 cts per yd & flannel from 60 to 75 & 80 cts per yd that is certainly a third higher than it used to be. now Pa gets two dollars a day like he used to when every thing was down as low as it has ever been but ten dolls now will not go as far in buying some things as five used to. Wages have raised but not as much as some other things. Pa is sometimes most discouraged for carpenter work comes very hard to him in the winter season, he has to be so much exposed & he is getting old & cannot stand as much as he used to. I shall look for Uncle Moses down this week & Matt will come with him but don't know as she will stay if she can make any thing up there she will not. Asher Smith is building a new house, he raised the frame while I was up to Grandpa's. Lewis has got that school at home this winter. Hiram Smith got it for him he can now be at home nights to see to things & that will make it easier for Grandmother. I am so glad for she is very much broke down & it is too hard for her to have to oversee the outdoor chores. I hope that I shall have a letter from you before I write again. I must stop now so good night.

Your ever loving mother S.R. Church
G.W.W.

Hospital No 2 Paducah, Ky
Nov 16th 63

My Dear Mother
it has not been but a few days since I wrote to you but as you have not heard from me very often lately I thought I would commence this morning & write you a good long letter. in the first place I will tell you how I am geting along. I think I am better than I was when I came here. I aint near as weak as I was. coming down the river on the boat made me a good deal worse & by the time we got here I was pretty weak. there was so many on the boat that we had no chance of geting any thing to eat. I got me some bread & butter the night we got on the boat that lasted me for supper and breakfast & that was all I eat till I came here & we were four nights on the boat so you may bet I was slim when I got here. as soon as I took a good wash & got on some clean clothes & got something inside of me I felt better right away. the first thing the Dr give me when I came here was castor oil & Turpentine rather a nasty dose but it done me good. after I took that a day he give me some kind of powders. I believe he is a good Dr. I am well suited with the place now but I may be tired of it before I get out of it. I think I can content myself here this winter very well. if I don't get no worse I will be satisfied & if I get well I will be willing to go back to the Regt. likely I will be here the most of the winter. I would try for a furlough now but they don't give any furloughs now. they did give them a short time before we came here but there was an order issued against it for the present. the day I came here there was only about 20 convalesents here & the next day the Hospital was filled up. there is now about 200 mostly convalesents. there is not but a few but that is able to get around. those that are not able to be around they put in a room by themselves & take all their clothes away from them but their drawers and shirts. they dont allow any clothes to lay around in the sick room. the day I came here there was no one in that room & they put me & two others in there but they let us keep our pants & shoes and blouse. I told them I could not lay abed all day & some days I did not feel like setting up all day. they told me I could stay in that room & if I wanted to lay down any through the day I could do so.. well the next day that room was filled with sick. I stayed in that room a day or two & yesterday I felt pretty well & was up all day & there was a fellow

stayed up stairs that was not able to help himself so they brought him down
& put him in my bed while I was out. well in the evening when I went to
go to bed I found it occupied. so I had to change my abode but I am well
suited with the change for I hate to be around where there is sick and some
one is up all night & they have a light burning all night so I could not half
sleep. I was very glad to make the change. I have just as good a bed & can
lay down when I please. I think I will get along fine now I have got a good
place to stay & a little different climate than I have been used to & a little
nearer the United States. I expect you will feel uneasy about me for I have
not had no chance to write much lately. I have not heard from home but
twice since we left Memphis. our brigade will be apt to see a hard time this
winter. I got away in a good time but I hated to leave the Co but I could
not go with them. Shermans Corp crossed the Tenn river at Eastport,
Alba & is going to march through to Chattanooga. our brigade is under
his command now. we got to Eastport two days before Shermans corps got
over & we did not leave Memphis for three weeks after he passed through
there. if he is that slow on foot he wont get to Chattanooga before spring. I
am not very well posted in the Army movements now for I have had no
chance to read the papers much lately. I have seen most of the election
returns & I am happy to know the Citizens went such a majority for
Brough. it is all right now. there was 9 Val voters in our Regt. I have wrote
to Arthur & he will remail all my letters & send them to me. we ought to
get mail in five days time now from each other. this is as near home as I
have been since I left. we expected to go on up to Louisville but the river
was so low we could not get transportation. we had a great time coming
down the river. our boat had another one in tow loaded with cotton &
reffugees. the boat was loaded to the guards & our boat had no load on &
the wind blew very hard & the river was very rough so both boats was in
danger. our of being blowed over and the other of sinking so we lashed
togeather. well we was coming round a bend in the river & the wind blowed
us right into an old tree top & came very near tearing the whole cabin off
the other boat. well in about an hour the old thing began to sink & such
climbing off I never saw. there was about 50 women & children on it but
they was not long in geting off. they headed for shore & got in before she
sunk. they worked at the thing about three hours & fixed her up. Well I
have just had a good dinner & I will now finish my letter. we had as good

a dinner today as I would want to set up to. we had potatoes cabbage beef good baked beans boiled ham & a good apple pudding with nice dip to put on it. supper & breakfast is not much to brag on but we have as much as sick men ought to eat. well I don't know but I have wrote enough for one time such as it is so I will wind up. I would write to Mat but I don't know whether she is at Uncles yet or not. You must excuse poor writing for this is poor ink. for fear you will not get the other letter I will tell you how to direct. Hospital No 2, Paducah, Ky. you need not send any more stamps till I write for them. No more this time my love to you all.

Your son Geo. Waterman
S.R.C.

#104

Hospital No 2 Paducah, Ky
Nov 22/63

My Dear Mother,
this is the Sabbath day & I thought I could not employ my time better than by writing to you. generaly though the week when I feel well I am running around town but I have a little respect for the Sabbath & employ my time at something else. I had the sick head-ache all the forenoon & it is a cold raw day or I should have went to meeting. last Sunday we had preaching here. O how I would like to be at home today. I have never thought so much of home since I left as I have since I have been here. one thing I have not heard from home for about a month & that seems like a good while but that is not your fault. the last one I got was the one you & Mattie wrote at Grandpas. I got it the 27th of last month & answered it the same day. I shall look for one tomorrow or next day. I have had another bad spell of the diarrhea since I wrote before. for three days I was just running night & day with it & the medicine that they give me here did not do me any good so I happened to think of your recipe & I went & got the stuff yesterday & fixed me up some of it. I got it done about noon & commenced to put it down me. I was astonished at the affect it had on me. I commenced to feel better right off & I did not have to get up once through the night & today my bowels is perfectly easy. I have not had much of a trial of it yet but I

think it is excellent medicine. I seem to have spells of the diarrhea. sometimes I will not have it much for a week or two then it will come on me & I will have it for three or four days till I get so weak I cant hardly walk. I have to eat very light diet. the grub that they have here is not very good for the diarrhea. I went to market the other morning & got me a pound of fresh butter & a chicken. I got the chicken stuffed and baked it & it would have made you laugh to see me go for the chicken bread & butter. that kind of living seems to do me some good & as long as I have money I am going to live. I can get a chicken stuffed & baked for 25 cts & it will last me as long as it will keep. if I was at home I would not eat anything but bread and milk but I aint there. I am counting the months though very impatiently. I don't expect to do any more duty while I am in the servis. If I ever get out of the army then I will have some hopes of geting cured up. it aint the medicine I need as much as it is the right kind of diet. I could do some light work if I had the right kind of food to live on. something nourishing. but I cant get that in the Army. well my hands is so numb that I cant half write & I have wrote about all I can think of so I will draw my letter to a close. write as often as you can all of you. let me know if you have got that money of Mr. Lawrence yet. my love to you all. no more this time but remain

Your loving Son Geo Waterman
S R C

#105

Hospital No 2 Paducah, Ky
Nov 30/63

Dear Mother
I seat myself this morning to write you a few lines & I expect they will be few for I have nothing to write about. it has been so long since I have had a letter & there is nothing going on here worth writing about so it will not be much of a letter that I will get up this time still I will try & write once a week if I don't write more than two lines.
We have been having a very cold spell of weather for a few days past but we have fared very well. there is only ten stays in the room that I do & we

have been permitted to have a fire. you better believe I stuck mighty close to the stove. coal is very scarce here. it is 75cts per bushel & cant get much at that. the river is raising & I am in hopes they will get on a good supply of fuel. one good thing I have a good warm room to sleep in & a first rate bed. as long as I am able to take care of myself I will get along very well. I am about the same I was when I wrote before. I feel tolerable well but I am poor & weak. I stick to the house tolerable close in cold weather for the wind cuts right through me in a cold day. I have no doubt but you worry about me but I don't want you to for I write just exactly how I am every time I write. I look worse than I feel for I am so poor. the most trouble I have is in geting something to eat that will agree with me. I have a tolerable good appetite but I eat very light of everything & I feel a good deal better by it. the less I eat the better I feel.

I begin to feel anxious to hear from home. it has been over a month now since I have had a letter. I am looking every day for one but it dont come. it will be hailed with joy when it does come. it has been most three weeks since I wrote the first letter from here & I think I ought to get an answer now before long. I know it aint your fault for you will write as soon as you get my letter. I want you to write all the news a week or two back. tell me where all the family is for they have been scattered so much lately that I don't know whether they have got them gathered up again. well I have wrote about all I can think of. you must excuse my short letter & when I get a letter I will have something to write about. for the present believe me your ever loving son

Geo Waterman

Hospital No 2 Paducah Ky Dec. 6th/63

Dear Mother,
I have at last got a letter from you & it was the most welcome letter I have received for I was so anxious to hear from home. It was just one month & five days since I received this last one so you may bet I was glad to hear from home & to hear that they were all well. I am a good deal better than I was when I wrote last. I have got the diarrhea checked on me & I feel tolerable well now any more than I am weak yet. All I want is something

nourishing now & I think I would soon pick up some. If I had the money I would board out at some favorite house. You say you are afraid if I don't get well. I don't expect to get rid of it as long as I am in the army. When I get home (if I ever do) then I will have some hopes for getting well. There ain't as much danger of this running a fellow into the consumption as the lung fever or the liver complaint. I think my livers is affected some now. I am very weak about the pit of my stomach & my breast is very weak. I believe I ought to take some kind of stomach bitters. This chronic diarrhea affects a man all over. He is all out of whack when he has it & it works very curious on a fellow. He can keep it stoped for about a week when it will break lose and run him nearly to death for a few days & then it will drop off. I have a very queer appetite. If I can't get just what I want I can't eat anything & I don't want one thing two days at a time. I buy nearly half I eat but I can't do it much longer for my pocket aint very deep and I haven't got my descriptive roll here so I can't draw my pay.

There was an agent came here last night from Ohio & they say he is going to get the names of all the Ohio soldiers there is in the hospital here and have them sent to their own state. I hope it is so. If I should have the good luck to get up north I would stand a good chance to get to go home. A man came here the other day after his son & he has to go to Columbus, Ky to get his furlough. This Dr. here has no authority to give a furlough or to discharge a man. If there was a chance for either one I would try.

I don't know about this mustering out troops three months before their time is out. I have heard such talk several times & a good many believes that they will. For my part I don't make any calculation on it. I will be out when my time is out any how.

We had an examination here the other day and them were able was sent to their regt. When the Dr. looked at me he said I was most too puny to go into the field yet. He would keep me here awhile yet.

Tell Freddy that I can't tell him when the war will be over or when I will go home but he need not be afraid of being drafted. We are having delightful weather for the time of year. It has been almost like spring for a few days. Well I have wrote about all I can think of so I will close. If you have not missed any letters you will know there is $30 at E. Lawrences for you. No more at present but remain your loving Son Geo. Waterman.

Hospital No. 2 Paducah, Ky
Dec 9/63

Dear Mother.
I have just received some letters from you that has been to the Regt &
remailed & sent back. one was written in Oct & the other was No 22. In
it you mentioned about L. Mitchell wanting me to pay half of that note.
You done right in not drawing the money for him. let him talk to Arthur
about that affair. I have nothing to do with it. I know my name is on the
note but let them get it out of me if they can. I am soldiering now & have
not time to attend to such things. so I would like to have them keep their
shirts on for a while yet. it makes me mad to be duned all the time. he has
wrote to me three or four times for money & I have sent it to him & now
he goes to you & wants you to draw the money out of the bank for him.
nice arrangement, he must think I am made of money. I expect he will nab
that $30 that I sent with Arthur. now Arthur acts the man about it. since
we failed to pay for the mill he has refused to accept me as a partner &
says I shall have to pay for what time I worked there & have what I have
paid toward the mill back again. I told him I had went into it & was
willing to stand my share of it. he said we had not made a written
agreement & he would not hear to me going in with him. then I told him I
never would take anything for what work I done but if he was bound to
pay me I would take what I had paid out for the mill which is $75 or $80.
to tell the truth I will be glad to get off at that. he wants to take the load
all on his own back & that is the reason why I want to help him. I will
write to Arthur & have him write to L.M. & tell him how the thing
stands. I thought he had done it before this. I think it is strange that
Mitchell would get sued on a note of Arthur & mine. I dont see into it. I
have been mad as a hornet every since I read the letter. in the first place
that confounded lie that E. Lottridge told made me mad & then I went on
& read this & it did not help me any. it has not been but three days since
I wrote but I thought I would set down & tell you how the thing was. such
stuff as she told never once entered my head & I am happy to know that

you all have too good sense to credit the story. I will admit I have wrote a few letters to her but I was ashamed of it. I worked there about two weeks & they was very anxious for me to write to them. well I done so & quit as soon as possible too. I will tell more about it when I get home. that girl done her best to get in with me but I kept my distance. You need not say anything about it so it will get out for it will only start another story. I was sorry to hear of Grandpa's death but I was looking for it when I heard he was sick. he was so old I knew he could not stand another sick spell. I received another letter from Rhoda & Lydia which I will try to answer tomorrow. it is getting late & I must begin to think of stoping. I am still gaining a little but have the diarrhea some yet. I received a few lines from Arthur today. they were at Elk river repairing the R.R. they were not in that late fight with Sherman. well I will stop for tonight & write to the girls tomorrow. so good night.

from your loving son
Geo Waterman
S C

Hospital #2 Paducah, Ky
Dec 16/63

Dear Mother.
I received a letter from you a few days ago but I see by the numbers that I have missed one. the first one I received here was No 25 & this one is 27. I am glad we took to numbering our letters for we can tell when one is missed. I have been bothered some with the diarrhea for a few days but have got it about stopped now but I have got an awfull sore mouth. if it was not for that I would feel tolerable well. we have made a change in Drs here & I like this one the best. he is more kind & attentive. I believe when my descriptive roll comes I will apply for a furlough. I don't expect I could get one but there is no harm in trying. I dont think to take the thing on an average that I am geting well very fast. I just about hold my own. this Dr seems to think I have the Dyspepsia & I would not wonder if I have for my stomach is very weak & it aint everything that will stay in me when I eat it. I eat bread & milk much as half the time. there is a woman that

sells milk here & a pint makes me a good meal. milk is 10cts a qt. here. Mother if you have not put that money in the bank yet when you get this I wish you would send me back a five dollar bill. I do hate to send for it after I have sent it home you must not think me a spend thrift Mother for God knows the most I spend goes to keep soul & body together. My descriptive roll wont get here time enough for me to draw pay this time so it will be two months after this month till I will get any pay but I will then get 2 months pay & will send some of it home.

I wrote to Arthur about that affair & told him to write to Lafayette about it also to me. We are having a good deal of wet & disagreeable weather here now but thank fortune I have a good warm place to stay & I stay pretty close too. You wanted to know if I had an overcoat. I have & plenty of other clothes to keep me comfortable & a good warm bed to sleep in. I have a straw tick quilt & sheet to lay on & a sheet two blankets & a coverlid over me it makes me think of home to get into that kind of a bed. your letters comes here in five days. it don't make many difference whether you put the co & Reg on or not. I see one of your letters had it on & the other did not. all the difference it makes is if I should not be here they will remail it & send it to the Regt. but they have my address any how so they would know. C. Atkinson had better luck in going home than I did. Perhaps it was on account of his child. it wont do for me to get homesick so I think as little of it as possible but still I would like to be at home this winter. you said you sent six postage stamps. I did not get but three but I think Arthur took the others to remail my letters. I told him he could. that scrapbook I read through & left it at the house where I was staying at Memphis. I hated to do it but I did not know but I would have to march & if I did I would have to throw it away & I did not like to do that so I left it. I spent a good many lonely hours in reading it. I see by looking over this that I got on the wrong side of the paper but I guess you will see the mistake. Well I have written enough for one time so I will close, hoping this will find you all in the enjoyment of health & happiness I remain as ever your loving son Geo Waterman

PS If Calista says anything about me not writing to her tell her that I don't feel so much & you are so near that they can hear from me & I feel myself bound to write to you if no one else.

GW

Camp Denison Ohio
Dec 23rd/63

Dear Mother.

Well I have made another move & this hitch I have got in the state of Ohio. the 19th of this month we were ordered to get ready to go to Ohio, well you better believe we were not long in geting ready to go. we took a boat from Paducah & came up to Evansville Ind. We stayed in the Hospital there overnight & the next morning we took the Cars for Cinti. we got here about 4 oclock last evening. I was very near tired out when we got here & I feel but little like writing this morning but I thought I must write some. in my last letter I wrote for some money. you need not send it now till I write again. I hope you have not sent it yet. I am so glad I have got this near home but there is no chance of getting any farther now for they don't give any furloughs. I wish when you write you would let me know if there is a Military Hospital at Galiopolis & if there is I will try & get transferred to it. well I will not write any more at present but will write in a few days & give you the particulars. I just thought I would write a few lines to let you know where I was, direct to General Hospital Camp Dennison Ohio Ward 14 .

#101

Camp Denison Ohio
Dec 26th/63

Dear Mother.

You may be surprised by receiving another letter from me so soon but this is all I have to do & so I was looking over your letters I see where you mentioned that you would like to send me some things if you had the chance. Well I have been thinking of it & it wont cost much to send me a small box of things & I will tell you what I want. I want a can of peaches for one thing & if you have any small cans of preserves that you think

would be good for me you may send it. my appetite craves something fresh
& juicy. if you can get it I would like to have about 1 1/2lbs of butter if
you can get some fresh. get a box about a foot sq & put in what you think
would be good for me & if I have any shirts you may put in two if I aint
mistaken I have some hickory shirts & I can wear them for under shirts. I
have two shirts but they are thin so I thought I would have you send me
some, it wont cost much to send the box but I don't know which way to
have it expressed. by river or RR. I expect it would be the best way to send
it to Athens by the hack. I would get it quicker & I want it for a New
Years gift. that is the reason why I wrote so soon again lots of the boys have
sent for such things & I don't want to be an odd one. you may pay for the
Expressing of it or not just as you are a mind to but if you do you must
take it out of my money. I can tell by the 10th of next month whether I
will be paid this time or not. If I don't I shall send home for some so if you
have not put that money in the bank yet you may keep out $5.00.
I begin to feel a little better than I did when I came here. I had the diarrhea
very bad when I got here but I have got it stoped now but I am still weak.
there is no prospect now of me going back to the Regt till my time is out. I
am sure to be put in the Invalid Corps & do Hospital duty when I am
able. they have just put a lot into it & there will be another examination
sometime next month. I expect to be put into it if I am able. I never will be
able to go to the field again & I don't care much what I do the rest of my
time out. My soldiering is over with any how. the first chance I see to get a
furlough I will put in for one. it will not take me long to go home from here.
they will give leave of absence for five or six days but it would not pay me
to get one for that length of time. I will wait till they give furloughs. I am
very well satisfied now for it seems almost like being at home to be this
close. I received that telegraph the day before we left Paducah. I was very
glad to get it. I read every word in it. I don't care if you send one every
week or two. We had a very Christmas dinner yesterday such as cakes
chickens & pies. I was very well satisfied with it concidering the chance we
had. tell C. Atkinson if he is there yet to stop & see me if he can when he
goes back. I expect he is gone though by this time. I can draw plenty of
clothes here but what I don't draw you know I get the money for when we
settle up so I don't intend to draw more than I can help & they aint
particular what kind of shirts a fellow wears. well I will close. I have wrote

more now than I thought I could when I commenced but I feel pretty well this morning.

My love to you all your loving son   Geo Waterman

PS if you have a small tin can with a cover on it put the butter in it so I will have something to keep it in. don't send a very large box but o hurry up the peaches

your hungry boy

Letter from Sophronia

Dec.30th/63

No 31

My Dear Boy,

 I have been busy all day to get things fixed to fill a box for you. I got your letter last evening. I was looking for it for you said in the other that you would write again in a few days. I expect you got one from me last night too, you ought to get one any how for I put one in the office Sun evening. I have put in two small cans of peaches & one of Quinces. They were stewed until they were soft & then sugar put in to sweeten them for use. I put up some without sugar and now I cannot tell which they are. I have put in a pound of loafsugar so if they are not sweet you can do it yourself. I have some to use on the peaches & it is better for your coffee too. I put in a little tin box of sweet pickled quinces, I think they will be good for you if you will not eat too much at a time & eat with something else, your bread and but will relish better with some such things. There is a still smaller box of jelly, in the bottom of the box there is cherry jelly & the top is grape, I put a little cloth in between and the corners are out so that you can take it out n get to the other when you want. I bought a tin box for butter and filled it but it is not as good as I wanted to get, but it is not strong. I had some maple sugar in the house so I took some of that & made some molasses for a variety. Aunt Laura sent me a nice cheese when Matt came home & I did not cut it until a few days before Christmas. I thought then how I wish that I would send George some but I had no idea that I should have a chance to before it was gone. I have put in a piece of it & I want

185

you to be careful & not eat but a little at a time. Mattie sent you a book. Mrs. Rhoda sent two red apples. I have put in some russets, now before you eat these things I want you to ask your Dr. how you ought to do in eating these things. I have heard of some that had been sick some time & got such as these & could not govern themselves & ate too much & did not live but a little while after. Now do George be very careful, a little will not hurt you, but your stomach is very weak & will not bear but little. Since I have been writing & since I have got the box almost full Mrs. Watson came over with a roll of butter and a few apples that they got of Mr. Horton, you will know them for they are not russets, she said she would make you a present of them.

You can roast some of the apples for a change. The girls wanted to make a cake but I would not let them now for I am afraid it would not do for you to eat rich and sweet food they was very unwilling to give it up. I told them that I would see how you got along with this & if you could govern yourself this time. I would send another after a while. I looked over your things and could only find one shirt to send so I put in one of Pa's old ones, it pretty good and we fixed it some so it will last some time. He has new ones so he will not want it. I will caution you once more, that when you think that mother would say stop, that is the time to stop. I have been making more inquiries about the hospital at Galipolis and find it an excellent place. They have women to cook & fix up things for those that have poor appetites & take it to their rooms for them and they say that they have an excellent Dr. L Atkinson is there yet, by his sisters tell he is very much like you are. I have got my paper full so I must stop. Your mother S.R. Church (I have not got your money yet)

#111

Camp Dennison Ohio
Dec 31st/63

Dear Mother
I received your letter of the 27th yesterday. it was mailed the 28th & I got it on the 30th. I am glad it is so we can hear from one another so soon. I am very glad I have got here. I have better care taken of me than I have had

any where I have been. they diet me here & that is what I need more than medicine. they feed me on scalded milk & light bread all the time. I begin to feel better now. I got the diarrhea stoped on me soon after I came here & it has not bothered me any since & I begin to feel a little stronger than I did. I have tried to get transferred to Galiopolis but could not do it. I think there will be no chance of it at all. you spoke of coming to see me. I would like the best kind to see you, but I am afraid it would be most to hard a trip on you & you would find poor accomodations unless you could get to stay at some friends house. I thought when I first read your letter I would write for you not to come but you may do as you think best. God knows I want to see you bad enough & I guess there will be some way for you to stay if you get here. if you come you had better not start with less than $20 & you may take it out of my pile. there is one thing I want you to bring me if you can come & can get the clear stuff & that is a bottle of currant wine. it is the best thing I could drink to strengthen me up. the Dr gave me ale but I would rather have currant wine. I did not think of it when I wrote for that box, I shall look for it tomorrow & then I shall have a good feast. I see by the number of this letter there is two letters I have not received but they went to Paducah first & I have written back there for them to send my mail to me. it has been such a short time since I wrote that I cant think much to write about now. I cant hardly realize yet that I am in a free country & among white folks. I feel perfectly contented now. only one thing lacks to make me happy & that is to see you all again. I am glad it gives you so much joy for me to get here. I am thankful for the change myself. if you conclude to come & Pa has nothing to do & thinks it would not cost too much why bring him along too I would like to see him as well as any of the rest & you could get along better with him with you & I will pay for one of you so it wont cost any more. well I have wrote all I can think of so I had better stop. My letters are short but they come often. hoping this will find you all well I remain

     your loving Son, Geo Waterman

     S R Church

You need not put General Hospital on the letters just put Camp Dennison Ohio. Ward 14 Send me a few stamps in your next letter.

10

INTRODUCTION TO THE 1864 LETTERS

*"But if you could make me a visit of a few days without inconvenience to
yourself I would be very much gratified."*
– George W. Waterman, January 15, 1864 (Ward 14)

*George Waterman's worldly possessions on the day
of his death*

On January 15, 1864, George Waterman, now weakened with illness, procured help from one of his nurses to pen a letter to his dear Mother. Little did he or the ward nurse know they were writing his last letter when asking her to visit. In the latter part of January 1864, Sophronia Church traveled from Pomeroy, Ohio, to the military hospital at Camp Dennison near Cincinnati, Ohio, to comfort her son. On January 31, she posted a letter to family back home with news of his slow recovery, expressing hope of bringing him there soon. George Waterman died just one day later on February 1, 1864.

The cause of death was an ulcerated bowel as a result of chronic diarrhea. Ignorance of the causes (primarily unsanitary conditions) and lack of proper medical treatment for infectious diseases such as typhoid, cholera, and dysentery led to the majority of Civil War deaths. Thus, George Waterman's was unremarkable in the annals of Civil War casualties. Waterman's 39th regiment of 881 lost a total of 196 men during the war: two officers and sixty-two enlisted men were killed or mortally wounded. Three officers and 129 men succumbed to disease – twice the number of combat fatalities.

For members of company K, George's loss was one of many deaths occurring in 1864. General Sherman's Atlanta campaign began on May 7 with the battle of Resaca, Georgia, commencing on the 9th. Nathan King was killed at Kennesaw Mountain in June and Martin Chambers at Nickojack Creek on July 5. Four others were killed at Atlanta on July 22, including George's friend Henry Knowles. If still with his command, George would have mourned the loss of his cousin Arthur Lawrence the most. Lawrence, also wounded during the July 22 assault, died a month after the battle on August 24.

Atlanta fell on September 2, setting the stage for Sherman's March to the Sea. George Waterman's future brother-in-law Alonzo Simms of the 33rd OVI participated in the march, collecting souvenirs along the way. Affixed to a small chain, these artifacts are now in the Schwartz family collection. At war's end the 39th and Fuller's Brigade were sent to Louisville, Kentucky, where they were mustered out on June 28, 1865.

Loss and heartbreak continued to follow Sophronia later in 1864 when her daughter and George's favorite sister, Martha "Mattie," died in November, two months after marrying William McMasters.

Sophronia's second husband Samuel Church died in 1889. She outlived two husbands and six of her nine children, dying in 1900 at age 84. Frederick Church ("Little Freddy"), her only child with Samuel Church, died in 1925.

Skeels private family cemetery, George Waterman's final resting place outside of Coolville, Ohio

Mary Schwartz, daughter of Francis Schwartz, standing with George Waterman's headstone in the Skeels cemetery

George Waterman was interred in the small Skeels family cemetery just outside of his boyhood home of Coolville, Ohio. He was buried alongside his great-grandfather Elijah Skeels and grandfather Sylvanus Skeels, who preceded him in death by just three months in November 1863. His sister Mattie joined him in eternity nine months later in November 1864; his grandmother Calista in 1876. The only other person to be buried in this hallowed resting place was George's Aunt Jane Skeels in 1898.

Little did George Waterman know that 155 years later, the chronicles of his war experiences, heartfelt and candidly written, would be published and shared all over the world.

190

11

THE 1864 LETTERS

The Last Letter

Ward 14 January 15, 1864

My Dear Mother,

I have not been able to write for some time and least you should suffer undue anxiety have concluded to employ a secretary.

The Dr. attending pronounces my case ulceration of the bowels. This medicine seems to operate favorably but I have got very weak.

He has taken my name for a discharge and if every thing goes favorably may expect to be at home in a few weeks.

But if you could make me a visit of a few days without inconvenience to yourself I would be very much gratified.

I do not suffer any pain am only weak. I like our Dr. very much and have full confidence in him and have every attention that circumstances will permit.

I sent my money to the bank subject to your order if you should decide to come you had better start with no less than $50.

I need only add that I remain Truly your affectionate Son George Waterman

---

A Letter from Sophronia home

Camp Dennison
Jan 31/64

To all at home,
This Sun. Morning I have just finished a letter to send to Mother, now I
will write one to send to you by the same mail. George is still mending very
slowly but I hope will continue to gain until I can get him home. I am
afraid that I shall get impatient staying here so long but I shall stay till I
can take him with me. I have a very good place to sleep, but a very hard
bed. I think that I am getting used to it now. I can sleep better than when I
first came here, it is very still here nights, they don't allow any loud talking
after nine oclock, they turn down the lights at half past eight. there is a
soldier here that was shot in the head at Gettysburg. he is given over by five
Drs, he has not been sensible much of the time for more than a week, his
sister came the same day that I came, she got here just at dusk. she is a
great deal of company for me & we stay in the ward Masters side quarters
at night. the ward Master is a very kind hearted man. he was George's
nurse, he wrote those letters for him. He was so pleased when I came. I
boarded here in the Matron's department. it is called the Drs. table, or the
diet room. They have plenty to eat, oysters nearly every day. George has
them nearly every meal. he is very fond of them & the Dr says that they
are good for him. Oysters & tapioca pudding is about all he eats now. This
camp is a beautiful place it is intirely level & is laid out in walks & in
front of the Wards is set out to all kinds of evergreens & flowers. in the
summer time they say it is a perfect flower garden here. they have very nice
shade trees set out. they have porches to every ward & they train Morning
Glories all over them. they have a very large Flower pit here, I have been to
it once but the sash was not off them. I shall try to see it open before I go
home if I can.
There is 75 wards here & from 5 to 6,7 & 8 in a Division. there is 5 in
our Division, the Dr says there is 2200 beds in all. some wards are
unoccupied now, every examination day there is some sent to their regiment
& some discharged & no new ones brought in for some time, I wish I could
tell how soon I could go home but I cant now, but as soon as I can I shall
let know immediately. I want you to write as soon as you get this if you

have not done so today. remember I am in a Camp now & want to hear from home & know how you get along & hear the news if there is any there was a man killed on the railroad Fri evening about seven oclock he is buried today by the Invalid Corps. That other sick man is better today he is sensible now & can talk some. George thinks he has got a little cold in his head today & does not feel quite so well this afternoon but I think it is nothing serious, he thinks he will be better tomorrow again. I shall wind up now for it is most time for me to send it out I will write again in a day or two, you will hear from me often while I stay. no more this time

Your Mother

S.R. Church

Tell Freddy that George says that he will bring him something. I will put this in an envelope that George had printed for a long time.

EPILOGUE

"Those who deny freedom to others, deserve it not for themselves."
– Abraham Lincoln

It is this writer's firm belief that the American Civil War was an unavoidable last resort to renounce and remove the practice of 250 years of slavery.

The policy of terror – capturing and removing millions of Africans from their homeland (with no common language with their captors) and enslaving them in a distant country – was not sustainable in an ostensibly free and democratic society. It took the bloodiest war in U.S. history to remove the degrading and violent yoke of human bondage. The abject misery that permeated the life of a slave was not entirely ameliorated by emancipation, but it was a start – "a new birth of freedom."

Over 600,000 young men, approximately 2 percent of the population, lost their lives in the Civil War. But as noted by historian Barbara Fields, the carnage of the war must make it about "something higher, about humanity, about human dignity. ..."

The polite, insightful Private George Waterman fought on the right side of history, and gave his young life – and his mother, her son – for the advancement of human freedom.

BIBLIOGRAPHY

Most of the documentation of the family history noted under the first chapter of this book can be found in the online Ancestry.com tree for Mary Schwartz. The federal land transactions for Skeels and Waterman are recorded on the General Land Office website: www.glorccords.blm.gov. The lineage of Samuel Waterman, grandfather of Private George Washington Waterman, is documented in *The Waterman Family* by Donald Lines Jacobus. Family member Mary Schwartz holds numerous family records and photographs, some of which have been added to the Ancestry.com tree. Land transactions are recorded in the Meigs County Courthouse and can be found online at *FamilySearch*. The service of Luther Waterman is documented in *Medical Men of the American Revolution* by Louis C. Duncan online at: https://history.amedd.army.mil/booksdocs/rev/MedMen/default.html. The pension file of Sophronia Church for the service of her son, George W. Waterman, Certificate number 224,789, Case Files of Approved Pension Applications, 1861–1934; Civil War and Later Pension Files; Record Group 15: Records of the Department of Veterans Affairs, National Archives, Washington, D.C., provides much of the information about George and also includes twelve of the letters he wrote to his mother. Additional information was obtained from family records and oral histories provided by George Waterman's descendant Francis Schwartz.

Additional sources have been provided below:

Bancroft, George, *Memorial Address on the Life and Character of Abraham Lincoln,* Washington Government Printing Office, 1866.

Barrett, Joseph H., *Life of Abraham Lincoln,* Moore, Wilstach and Baldwin, New York, 1865

Chernow, Ron, *Grant,* Penguin Press, New York, 2017

Delbanco, Andrew, *The War Before the War,* Penguin Press, New York, 2018

Dyer, Frederick H., *A Compendium of the War of the Rebellion. 3 Volumes,* Thomas Yoseloff, New York, 1959

Grant, Ulysses S., *Personal Memoirs of U.S. Grant,* Charles Webster and Co., New York, 1885

Guelzo, Allen, *Lincoln's Emancipation Proclamation,* Simon and Schuster, New York, 2004

Keesee, Dennis M., *Too Young To Die, Boy Soldiers of the Union Army,* Blue Acorn Press, Huntington, West Virginia, 2001

Lepore, Jill, *These Truths A History of the United States,* W.W. Norton and Company, New York 2018

Livermore, Thomas L., *Numbers and Losses in the Civil War in America 1861-1865,* John Kallman, Carlisle, Pa. 1996

Long, E.B., *The Civil War Day by Day, An Almanac 1861-1865,* Double Day & Co. New York, 1971

Lossing, Benson J. *History of the Civil War and the Causes That Led Up to the Great Conflict,* Published by the War Memorial Association, 1912

Nichols, Clifton M., *Life of Abraham Lincoln,* Mast, Crowell and Kirkpatrick, New York, 1896

Ohio, 1860 Census records, Microfilm Division, National Archives, Washington D.C.

Ohio Roster Commission, *Official Roster of the Soldiers of the State of Ohio in the War of the Rebellion, 1861-1866,* 12 volumes, Akron, Cincinnati, Norwalk, 1886-1895

Reynolds, David, *John Brown, Abolitionist,* Alfred A. Knopf, New York, 2005

Smith, Charles H., *The History of Fuller's Ohio Brigade 1861-1865, It's*

Great March, with Roster, Portraits, Battle Maps and Biographies, J. Watt, Cleveland, 1909

Williams, H.Z. & Bro., *History of Washington County, Ohio: with illustrations and biographical sketches,* H.Z. Williams, Cleveland, Ohio 1881

Zinn, Howard, *A People's History of the United States*, Harper Perennial, New York, 1980

Made in the
USA
Lexington, KY